AF324638

The New Americans
Recent Immigration and American Society

Edited by
Steven J. Gold and Rubén G. Rumbaut

A Series from LFB Scholarly

Undocumented Students and the Policies of Wasted Potential

Janet K. Lopez

LFB Scholarly Publishing LLC
El Paso 2010

Library of Congress Cataloging-in-Publication Data

Lopez, Janet K., 1976-
  Undocumented students and the policies of wasted potential / Janet K. Lopez.
     p. cm. -- (The new Americans: recent immigration and American society)
  Includes bibliographical references and index.
  ISBN 978-1-59332-393-6 (hardcover : alk. paper)
  1. Latin Americans--Education (Secondary)--North Carolina--Case studies.
2. Illegal alien children--Education (Secondary)--North Carolina--Case studies. 3. Educational equalization--North Carolina--Case studies. I. Title.
  LC2670.4.L67 2010
  371.829'680756--dc22

                                        2010011830

ISBN 978-1-59332-393-6

Table of Contents

Acknowledgements

The completion of this book has been a long journey but one I considered a great privilege. I am thankful to all the people who supported me through personal and professional levels of support.

I would first like to thank all of the students who participated in this research. They opened their lives and their hearts to me so that their stories could be shared with the academic world. They made themselves vulnerable so that people might read their stories and want to change the current reality. They did this for themselves but more so for their peers and the siblings who will follow after them.

I would also like to thank the teacher allies who participated in the research. They were first identified by the students, and it became obvious early into the research process the amount of blood, sweat, and tears each of them put into their jobs as educators.

There are many people who helped me through this research including Dr. George Noblit, Dr. Regina Cortina, Dr. Jim Trier, Dr. Bryan Brayboy, Dr. Peter Kaufman and Dr. Luis Urrieta. I would also like to thank peer colleague Dr. Courtney George. A special thank you is in order for Matt Gianneschi, Paul Lingenfelter, Hiroshi Motomura, Paz Oliverez and Michael A. Olivas. In addition to those who helped me think through these difficult issues, there were also those who helped me "do." Thanks you to my original copy editor Pat Gianneschi and additional editors Kate Broyles and James Bruski. Dalila Medina Rangel provided Spanish translations early in the research process. Research funding for the initial work on this book was generously provided by UNC/Duke Latin American Studies Consortium.

CHAPTER 1

Undocumented Students in North Carolina

The kids will find a way to get things. They are extremely resourceful, so that's why the college thing: sometimes I get down about it, and other times, I don't because the population is very resourceful and they have overcome things, all kinds of things. Every kid that you have met at that school has come across that desert, in some way they have crossed that desert. Sometimes the cross is easy; sometimes it's very difficult. Sometimes people barely managed to survive, so they have been through the fire in ways that other kids haven't, and they take it all in stride. It's a wonderful quality. -John, teacher

Today, statistics show that approximately 80,000 undocumented students reach high school graduation age every year in the United States.[1] The nearly 65,000 of them who will graduate, have also been living in the country for five years or more (Gonzales, 2009). The undocumented high school student population in the Southeastern United States is an

---

[1] This estimated number includes undocumented students from different countries of origin. This research focuses on Mexican-Origin immigrants, the largest immigrant group in North Carolina in 2007.

area of educational research that has received little attention. The Southeastern region is of interest because these states have the highest percentage of Latinos likely to be undocumented, and at the same time have no in-state tuition policies (Flores & Chapa, 2009). Information regarding Latino high school students is readily available in policy and research reports, however no official data regarding documentation status are collected in the public school systems at the state or federal level. For example, while the 2001 U.S. Census data reports that the majority of North Carolina's Latino population is foreign-born (61%), it can only estimate what percentage of them are undocumented. During the time of the research that constitutes this book it was estimated that nearly 1,500 undocumented students were graduating from North Carolina high schools each year (El Pueblo Inc., 2005).

Research conducted on undocumented high school students paints a picture of bright students who have displayed a great deal of resiliency and strength both in their journey across the border, their adjustment to American schooling experiences, and their perseverance in higher education (Albrecht, 2007; Barato, 2009; DeLeon, 2005; Perez et al. 2007; Rincon, 2008). These students have overcome numerous obstacles throughout their K-12 experiences and will confront many more during the college application process, despite their academic talents and abilities. Policies limiting their access to higher education often prevent them from going on (Oliverez, 2005a; Oliverez, 2005b; Perez, 2006). Although Plyer v. Doe (1982) holds that it is illegal for a state to deny school-aged undocumented students free public education, Section 505 of the Illegal Immigration Reform and Immigrant Responsibility Act (IIRIRA) bars undocumented students from receiving in-state tuition or federal financial aid. 10 states (California, Illinois, Kansas, Nebraska, New Mexico, New York, Oklahoma, Texas, Utah and Washington) have laws that allow undocumented students in-state tuition; the majority of states do not allow undocumented students to claim in-state residency (NILC, 2009).[2] And one state, South Carolina, has explicitly banned students from attending or receiving financial aid at public colleges (Gonzales, 2009).

In addition the economic barriers (Barrato, 2009; Flores, forthcoming 2010; Oliverez, 2005a; 2005b), research has found that

---

[2] In 2008 Oklahoma (HB 1804) rescinded its law for in-state tuition but left a clause that allows the Board of Regents to enroll a student in higher education institutions permitted that they meet special requirements.

undocumented immigrants face racial prejudices and discrimination regarding beliefs in their innate inferiority and inability to continue on towards higher education (Oliverez, 2005a; Oliverez, 2005b; Rincon, 2008). Along with the difficulty of often being first-generation and navigating the college and application process on their own (Oliverez, 2005a; Oliverez 2005b), undocumented high school students must also recognize that many in the American public see them as less deserving of public resources and "membership" in U.S. society (Murillo, 2002; Perry, 2006). While many undocumented high school students were brought to the United States through a broken immigration system, the attempts to access a college education may be their first encounter with the limitations imposed in the United States without proper residency status.

While previous research (De Leon, 2005; Olivas, 1995; Olivas, 2004; Olivas, 2005; Oliverez, 2005a; Oliverez, 2005b) had focused on undocumented high school students who live in states where they may access in-state tuition, in 2006 no research had been conducted in states where students were legally prohibited from in-state tuition. North Carolina is a state that does not provide in-state tuition for undocumented students and only created an official policy verifying that undocumented students could apply to the University of North Carolina's statewide system as out of state residents in 2004. The community college system in North Carolina has waffled back and forth on their policy since 2001, but in 2007 did allow undocumented North Carolina high school graduates to enroll and pay out of state tuition (Lee et al. 2009).

This book adds to the body of knowledge regarding undocumented high school students in the Southeastern United States, an area that has received little attention in the educational research community. As an ethnographic case study, it will focus on one high school with a large undocumented student population and the research will illuminate the lives of five high-achieving undocumented high school seniors and six teacher allies who encouraged undocumented students in this high school to obtain a college education.

Using Critical Race Theory (CRT) and Latino Critical Theory (LatCrit) frameworks, this book explores how access to higher education for undocumented Latino immigrants is shaped by issues of race and ethnicity and how inequities in public education continue to shape the education aspirations of Latino students. Using concepts from both CRT and LatCrit, including forms of resistance, counternarratives, and identity construction, the research will explore the experiences of undocumented high school seniors of Mexican-origin[3]: how policies regarding undocumented immigrants have created significant barriers for students who have lived much of their lives in the United States and who have maintained a strong academic record in preparation for education beyond high school. This book attempts to address the following questions:

- How do undocumented students navigate the public education system and attempt to navigate the higher education system?
- What are the counternarratives undocumented students provide to counter the labels of "problem" and "illegal alien" in their community?
- How have these students' demonstrated resilience and tactics of resistance in their educational trajectories?
- What value could undocumented students bring to the higher education system?
- How does being undocumented shape a student's identity?

Within the CRT framework, this case study will employ the construct of structural determinism (Delgado & Stefanic, 2001) and interest convergence theory (Bell, 1979; Bell, 1985; Bell, 1992; Bell, 2005) to discuss the constraints that adult allies (teachers, coaches, mentors) face when trying to help undocumented students access higher education. Chapters that incorporate the voices of the teachers will attempt to answer the following questions:

- What advice do teacher allies give to undocumented high school students?
- What goals are undocumented students encouraged to pursue after graduation?
- What do teacher allies believe keeps high achieving undocumented students in school if the opportunity to attend college is likely unobtainable?
- What approach does the school follow when working with undocumented students?

---

[3] The label Mexican-origin rather than Mexican-born was utilized because these students have lived in the United States for many years and have identities which are both Mexican and American. Mexican-origin rather than Mexican-born reflects that they were born in Mexico and identify with their Mexican-nationality but also have an American identity as well.

This book argues that undocumented students are severely challenged when attempting to access college opportunity, and that in the future the increase in the number of college-eligible students among this population will continue to grow. As a result, just when the U.S. needs more and more talented students and workers we are hobbling this potential resource. The research sheds light on the experiences of undocumented students in North Carolina who aspire to attend college, with emphasis on how the absence of in-state tuition policy deeply affects their chances for moving beyond second-class citizenship.

THE RESEARCH

In the fall of 2004 I began working as the director of a mentoring program at a large public research university in North Carolina. The mentoring program paired college students with high school students at Benson Guthrie High School (a pseudonym) in Sunder Crossings, North Carolina (a pseudonym). The program included Latino students at the high school attending events at the university as well as students at the university traveling to BGHS events. The program began in a student's sophomore year and followed the student through graduation, with the ultimate goal of attending a four-year university once the program was completed.

During my second year working for the program several of the teachers at the high school alerted me to a group of academically strong juniors who were too old for eligibility in our program, but who they believed would benefit from participation in the Latino Outreach events. Through trusting relationships with these students, the teachers knew that each of these students was interested in college but was also an undocumented immigrant and would find it extremely difficult to attend university in North Carolina. After meeting each of these students and gaining permission from them to participate in a research study, I began following these 5 students through their senior year of high school. All of them allowed me to follow their lives and track their academic progress through graduation day. In addition, several teacher allies (teachers who had encouraged the students in high school) were invited to participate in the research. This book is a result of my time with these individuals.

JOURNEYS TO THE UNITED STATES: A MOMENT OF INTRODUCTION

The five students who stepped forward to participate in this book risked sharing with another person their status in the United States as undocumented immigrants. All of them had their own unique journeys, yet they shared the common thread of families who leave Mexico: to escape poverty. Each family crossed the border with hope that the losses they faced in leaving their homeland would be eased by better paying jobs in the United States. To understand the resiliency these students exhibited in their American classrooms, we must first understand the physical hardship they undertook to make it to Sunder Crossings, North Carolina at all.

Carmen

Having crossed from Mexico into Arizona at the age of 11, Carmen noted that her brother and uncle were lost in the Arizona desert for several days, so that in comparison, her trip was not nearly as dangerous. The trip is burned deeply into her memory, and she re-told the story as though it were only last week (in reality it had been nearly six years). Somewhere near the border of Mexico, Carmen's journey began when two old ladies pulled up in a large van and instructed all of the children to sit in the back seats. Carmen and her cousin were shoved into one car seat. If the van was stopped, all the children were instructed to act as though they were in a "really, really, deep sleep." When the packed van arrived in the United States, they stayed in a crowded safe house for nearly three days. Carmen recalled that there were only two or three rooms in the house and that many people stayed inside the packed rooms, sleeping each night on the dirty carpet. Finally, another van, stuffed 16 with more than 16 people inside it, took them up through various states into North Carolina. Carmen insisted, "I promise it wasn't, like, that bad. I know people who had it much worse."

As a senior, this young woman was an active member of the BGHS community. She had been able to maintain her Mexican culture while still integrating successfully into the school. She was active in soccer, yearbook, and peer tutoring, and worked nearly 30 hours per week at a local fast food restaurant. She fought often with her parents about becoming more like American girls and had been kicked out during her spring semester to live with an aunt and uncle because her parents disapproved of her relationship with a serious boyfriend. Carmen maintained her Spanish as she improved her English, and scored a 5 on the AP Spanish placement tests. She dreamed of attending a private Catholic university or the University of North Carolina.

Frances

Frances' repeated border journeys had multiple entry points. As a small child, she recalled, violence between her parents erupted time and time again, so the decision to first cross the border was made for the family to get a fresh start. Since she had been no more than three years old, I assumed that she had no memory of that first crossing, yet she quickly corrected me, and began to share her story. Their first crossing involved the raging waters of the Rio Grande. While she couldn't remember where or when they crossed, the memory of clinging to her father's back and getting multiple scratches from low-hanging tree branches still resonated in her mind.

While there would be more trips back and forth to Mexico as her mother left from and returned to the violent relationship with her father, Frances's last trip was the result of great tragedy. Her father had been killed in a suspicious car accident (possibly the result of a drug deal gone bad), and not soon afterwards, her mother was struck down by illness. She and her brother, now young teens who were orphaned, were sent by their aunt in Mexico City to live with her aunt and uncle in Sunder Crossings. On this trip Frances and her brother departed from Tijuana and crossed the border in the car of a white college-age student. She remarks, "And we just crossed the border in the car, and they didn't even ask any questions. I guess we both just looked white enough."

Since Frances did not arrive in Sunder Crossings until the age of 15, she remained deeply connected to her Mexican heritage, and admitted that if she had to return, she could be happy back in Mexico. A strong student who had attended high school in Mexico City, Frances and her uncle fought to have her enrolled in the appropriate grade level when she entered BGHS as a junior. (Many of her counterparts had been placed back into the 9th grade regardless of their coursework in Mexico). During her two years in Sunder Crossing, she became active in a Latino advocacy group, contributed to a student-organized radio show, and helped to organize community events. A family friend who attended college was encouraging her to apply to university. Frances felt that a college education was a chance at a more independent life for a woman, and she wanted such a life.

Ricardo

With jet black hair and piercing dark eyes, Ricardo stared intensely at me as he described the anger at his situation. In Sunder Crossings since the age of seven, Ricardo had always been under the impression that he had some type of proper legal paperwork; he only found out, through a mishap during high school, that his stepfather's attempt to create a better life for him and his mother had included creating social security numbers for each of them, numbers that didn't really exist.

Ricardo recalled that, unlike many of his peers, his family had made it to the United States on their "first try". The trip had been relatively uncomplicated: walking across the almost dry river when it was the low season, walking for many more hours through the woods somewhere in Texas, checking into a hotel where they stayed for only a night or two, then getting onto a plane in Dallas with a direct flight to Raleigh, North Carolina. Ricardo's stepfather's investment in a reliable *coyote*[4] (sometimes upwards of $4000 per person), had been a worthwhile investment. Ricardo remembered his mother explaining to him what their new life was going to be like in North Carolina and says he didn't feel scared about making the journey to North Carolina or starting a new life in the United States.

As a senior Ricardo was an ESL tutor for the school. It was during this paid tutoring experience that a woman several counties over attempted to collect her retirement check, only to be told that she could not because the system indicated that she was working at a high school in a nearby county. Ricardo then learned that the social security number given to the school by his father was not his but a false number that actually belonged to this woman. Facing possible deportation and a criminal sentence because of his false social security number Ricardo continued to excel in his senior-level coursework, finishing in the top 11% of his class. While Ricardo was interested in attending college, he understood that, until he was able to "get papers," he would not be able to go to college.

Fidel

As a senior in high school, Fidel's painful memories of crossing over the border had been re-imagined and re-ignited once he realized that, because of his undocumented status, he would not likely be able to attend college. His family's difficult journey included being caught twice and thrown into a deportation jail after the second failed attempt. Fidel recalls their

---

[4] A *coyote* is a person that is paid to smuggle immigrants into the United States.

giving the border authorities fake names so that they could not track the family's attempts should they be caught again. When dropped off back in the state of Puebla after the second attempt, the family made a collective decision to attempt the crossing one final time.

On the third try, the family took a bus from Central Puebla to the borderlands of Mexico (about a 12 hour drive). Once they arrived at the border, they began walking through the night: this involved "walking, running, and hiding" at several points along the border. At the final step, the *coyotes* led the family to a tall fence where they had to climb over or be left behind. Fidel mentioned that his great fear of heights was a result of this moment, and he recalled the fear that engulfed him as he looked down toward the ground from the top of the fence. After arriving in Arizona, the family spent several days hiding in an abandoned house. After what seemed like an eternity to Fidel, the family headed to a local airport and flew to Raleigh, North Carolina.

Because he was one of the academic superstars of his high school, many teachers would have found it hard to imagine that Fidel's entry into the United States had been fraught with such danger. Since his arrival in the United States, he had been an outstanding student, taking seven of the nine AP courses offered at the high school. Fidel was somewhat estranged from the other Mexican students because he took coursework with almost all white students. At the same time he also felt somewhat alienated from the white population in his AP courses, who had no understanding of his family background. Fidel spent much of his time writing his thoughts into a novel. He had scored exceptionally well on his achievement tests, and the teachers felt he would be a competitive applicant to many colleges. He planned to apply to the University of North Carolina, his top choice, along with several other public and private colleges in the state that his research showed would accept undocumented students.

Saul

While all of the students' journeys represented difficult points in their lives, Saul's was unique, for his was traveled alone. At the age of 11, Saul's longing for a father who had left for *Carolina del Norte* years before became too much to bear, and Saul set off on his own to find his father. While his mother reluctantly agreed to let him travel with a cousin, Saul recalled the tears in his younger brother's eyes as he begged him not to go: "He said '*Hermanito, hermanito*, please don't go.' He said that if I left, he wouldn't have anyone to fight with." Despite his brother's pleas, Saul set out on a journey that would encompass more than 20 days to be reunited with his father.

Once Saul arrived at the border, the cousin's promise to take him across fell through, and after spending several days in a town near the border, he was able to convince a *coyote* to take him across on the promise that the *coyote* would collect half of his money once they arrived over the border via a money transfer from his father, and the other half when they arrived in North Carolina. As Saul described his journey in excruciating detail, this handsome, strong young man took breaks to wipe away tears. Saul described how he, only a boy was forced to walk for days on end, to share one can of tuna with four other travelers for a daily meal, to withstand freezing nights in the fields of Texas farms, to carry his own gallon jug of water in his small backpack, and to drink from animal troughs which sometimes contained feces and dirt.

Saul painfully described the shame he felt about sneaking through people's yards, the fear he felt when almost caught by border security, and the pain he felt when hunger overtook his body; it was an experience he never wanted to re-live. Yet, Saul recalled that even though he understood, even then that it was dangerous, the only thing he really cared about was being reunited with his father. Between praying and reminding himself of his father, he was able to withstand the difficulty of the journey. When Saul arrived in Sunder Crossings nearly 20 days after his departure from Mexico he rejoiced in recognizing the familiar face of his father, a face that looked like the mirror image of the younger brother Saul had left behind.

When he was a freshman, Saul and his father were finally joined by his mother and younger siblings. The pain of the journey was not forgotten but the strength and closeness of his family life was evident when I saw them together at Saul's soccer games at the high school. Saul was an outstanding soccer player and a student, who had challenged himself with Honors English, Calculus and AP Spanish. With the encouragement of several teachers in the school, Saul decided to apply to the University of North Carolina. If he was not accepted, he considered working for a couple years to help his family pay the bills and then re-applying to college if and when the state's laws change.

Allies in the Field: The Teachers
The six teachers in this book were identified by the undocumented students as those people within the school who had helped or encouraged

them to think about and apply to college. Because of the help they offered to the undocumented students and to other Latino students in the school, I have defined them as teacher allies. These teachers all have unique stories of their own, but in order to protect their anonymity since many remain as active members of the high school faculty and Sunder Crossings community, I only will provide a brief collective synopsis of their backgrounds. The six teachers included male and female teachers, all of whom played various roles in the school community beyond their required teaching duties. These teachers were student organization supervisors, sports coaches, and extra-curricular activity directors. They all lived inside or near Sunder Crossings, and they had all been in the school for at least three years. These teachers had reached out to the Latino community in ways beyond helping students consider colleges and their title of "ally" to the participants was well-deserved. They were the teachers who worked with the students every day, and while the federal and state governments set policies regarding access to higher education for students, they were the ones who dealt with those policies. As one teacher commented, "It's a mess, it's a mess and we have to live in the middle of the mess, and we had to help clean up the mess here, so it's very hard, it's very hard."

Soy Chicana: My Story
My story is not like theirs, yet I am part of them as well. I am Latino and white, the product of middle class suburbs and parents of mixed heritage. I am the child of a Chicano father whose family lost their native language in the quest to assimilate, a language which I now struggle to regain. I am also the child of a white mother who feels threatened by my passion for my Chicano heritage. I walk in many worlds: worlds into which many of my Latina/o counterparts with darker skin and stronger accents are not allowed to venture without fear of being detected. I am a mixed-heritage researcher.

I moved to North Carolina specifically to study the growing Latino population in the state. When I arrived, my background and research interests focused on high-achieving Latino students. Admittedly, I was basically unaware of how many undocumented students were in the public school systems nationwide. I had lived and attended school in only two states, both of which had long histories of Chicano roots and pride. New immigrant communities were outside my realm of experience. I also attended school and grew up in spaces where Latinos were powerful and had strong leaders in their communities, places with long Chicano histories. Arriving in North Carolina, I soon discovered how few Latino students, either undergraduates or graduates, attended college in the state. While I met several wonderful Latinas/os along the way, few of the undergraduates, graduate students, professors, or professionals in the community were Mexican-American. Few of the people I met in North Carolina had memories of Latina/os living in the state, save for the farm workers who picked crops. This was a completely new experience for me, for I came from states (Colorado and Texas) that had both belonged to Mexico before the United States.

When I started volunteering at BGHS I could not claim that I understood my students' experiences. Yet when I met the students at BGHS, I instantly felt a kinship to them. While our Latino backgrounds were extremely different, our shared academic identity as "high-achievers" was extremely similar. These were kids who, like me, had parents, who while still encouraging us to do our best in school, knew little about attending college. These students also had a select group of teachers who were doing everything possible to give them the capital to achieve higher education. As the director of the mentoring and college prep program that served BGHS' Latino community, I was given the privilege of working with many of the participants' friends, family members, and teachers throughout the period I was conducting research on these students.

APPROACHING THE RESEARCH

As an ethnographer, I am trying to understand how the policies and laws concerning undocumented immigrant students' access to higher education affect the individual students who are living each day as "illegal." During this journey, I not only researched the policies and laws particular to North Carolina and the nationwide, but I also spent time in the communities my participants lived in before arriving in the United States, and the place that they now call home. I have also observed the workplaces where both they and their parents often provide services and goods for the economy, and the activities that frame their daily lives inside and outside of school. This book emerges from my efforts to understand the meaning and significance of the policies in North Carolina that prohibit undocumented college-ready high school students from accessing higher education, as well as some of the national laws regarding unauthorized immigration to the United States. Through a framework of CRT and LatCrit theories, this book examines the structural limitations of continuing on to higher education created by the policies that currently exist in North Carolina.

Ultimately, the book highlights how policies currently in place in North Carolina severely limit what opportunities the students can create for themselves, how little teacher allies can assist these students, and how much the state is losing out on an opportunity to capitalize on the transnational knowledge and capital that undocumented students possess from their experiences of living in two cultures.

THE END AND THE BEGINNING

In the initial months when I began the research, I approached the Sunder Crossings school board regarding the opportunity to conduct direct observations in the classrooms at Benson Guthrie High School. The exchange that occurred between me and a high level administrator appears below:

Janet: Hi, Mr. Miller (a pseudonym) this is Janet Lopez the woman who applied to conduct research at Benson Guthrie High School. I just wanted to clarify some of the questions you had about my research. What I want to do is to conduct research with Latino high school students who are prepared to go to college, including those who are undocumented students.

Dr. Miller: Undocumented, oh you mean the kids who are 'illegal'; well we don't have any of those students at Benson Guthrie High School.

Janet: (Somewhat shocked, but recognizing that he may be trying to protect his students). Well, I have been working with the high school for a year and I think that there are students at BGHS who are in this situation.

Dr. Miller: Oh, I'm sorry I guess you misunderstand me, we might have some 'illegal' students at that high school, but *none* of them are capable of doing college level work.

Janet: Well, Mr. Miller I think some might disagree with your statement, but I'm hoping this research will figure out if they exist or not.

Dr. Miller: Well, you'll have to submit all the proper paperwork to gain access to that school, and I don't think you'll find any of those types of students at Benson Guthrie. That's all the questions I have for you, please submit your paperwork as soon as possible.

While some K-12 school officials living in Sunder Crossings, such as Mr. Miller, held deficit views about undocumented immigrants, I also ran into university officials who felt similarly. At one private university I contacted, the director of admission explicitly told me that their university made it a policy not to work with undocumented students, but that this was not often a problem because undocumented students rarely met the university's academic standards for admission. If this research provides no other evidence regarding undocumented student experiences', it should clearly prove that undocumented Mexican immigrant students have the academic ability and intellectual capacity, similar that of any of their other Black or White classmates at Benson Guthrie High School, to do the work and be successful at the university level.

This research brings voice to the undocumented student population, and brings much needed research regarding the importance of providing access to higher education for a long-neglected population of students. It is my hope that this book sheds light not only on students in North Carolina but on the thousands of undocumented students living in this country who are college-ready and have the ability to succeed, to contribute to the higher education community, and ultimately, if given the chance, to contribute to the global workforce in our country.

CHAPTER 2

Latino Experiences of Inequitable Education: Immigrant Children, Undocumented High School Students and North Carolina's Growing Population

This book is grounded in the literatures of Latinos in education (Moll, Amanti, Neff, & Gonzalez, 1992; Portes & Rumbaut, 2001; Portes, 2004; Stanton-Salazar & Spina, 2003; Stanton-Salazar & Spina, 2000; Stanton-Salazar, 2001; Valenzuela, 1999) high achieving Latinos (Conchas, 2006; Gandara, 1995; Lopez, 2004) and Latinos in higher education (Gonzalez, Stoner, & Jovel, 2003; Solórzano, Villapando, & Oseguera, 2005; Urrieta, 2003). The work also is grounded in the literature surrounding Latino immigrant experiences (Carreon, Drake, & Barton, 2005; Gibson, Gandara, & Koyama, 2004; Murillo, 2002; Olsen, 1997; Suárez-Orozco & Paez, 2002; Suárez-Orozco & Suárez-Orozco, 2001; Valdes, 1996; Wortham, Murillo, & Hamann, 2002), with a special emphasis on undocumented high school immigrants (Barato, 2006; De Leon, 2005; Flores, 2006; Olivas, 1995; Olivas, 2004; Olivas 2005, Oliverez, 2005a; Oliverez, 2005b; Perry, 2006). Within the discourse on undocumented immigrants I am also particularly interested in the literature that exists around the transnational student experience (Anzaldua, 1987; Trueba, 2004;

Trueba & Bartolome, 2000). My research is framed by policy reports and research that have highlighted the Latino experience in the South (Kasarda & Johnson, 2006; Tomas Rivera Policy Institute, 2005), and Latino student underrepresentation in higher education (Fry, 2002; Fry, 2004; Oliverez, 2005a; Passel & Fix, 2004; Protopsaltis, 2005). Finally, this research is framed by the discussion regarding the history of immigration law (Aleinikoff, Martin, & Motomura, 2003; Haney Lopez, 1996; Motomura, 2006; Ngai, 2004; Perry, 2006; Pickus, 2006).

The literature pertinent to this research falls into three categories. The first category includes a review the history of immigration law and policies. The second area includes the literature regarding Latino students in both K-12 and higher education. Since this research focuses on immigrant students of Mexican origin, whenever possible the literature highlights Mexican-origin specifically. Third, I review the literature concerning immigrant students paying particular attention to undocumented high school students and the transnational student experience. Policy reports and research regarding Latino issues particular to higher education and Latinos living in the South are also examined.

HISTORY OF IMMIGRATION LAW

Immigration law reveals in concrete terms our societal values and attitudes towards immigrants. These laws reflect negative American attitudes towards immigrants and what their role should be in American society. The history of immigration law shows that, over time, the courts defined a sense of who belonged and who did not. Historic immigration cases aimed to exclude certain racial/ethnic groups and, from the beginning, reflected an evolving sense "us" versus "them" (Motomura, 2006).

One of the first immigration laws, the Chinese Exclusion Act of 1882, created a moratorium on Chinese immigrants, whom many Americans considered dirty and suspicious. Chinese Immigrants comprised 90 percent of the work force that built the Central Pacific Railroads; Americans subjected these workers to a form of indentured servitude. Other immigration laws, including the Alien Enemies Act (1798) and the Nationality Law of 1898 (immigrants had to prove their citizenship by having a free white person of good moral character testify how long they had been in the country), made it incredibly difficult for Chinese immigrants to become citizens (Motomura, 2006). Over time anti-immigration sentiment, encouraged by nativists, restrictionists, and social Darwinists developed different arguments against bringing more immigrants not of European origin into the country: Supposedly, they diluted America's "pureness" and lowered American standards of living.

Political parties like the Know-nothings party, Theodore Roosevelt's attempt to "swat-the hyphen movement (i.e. Mexican-American or Chinese-American)," and the Americanization Curriculum (Gonzalez, 1990) were all concrete attempts to push a model of Americanism and to promote Anglo-Saxon superiority (Motomura, 2006). When the United States hired Mexican labor in the West and thousands of Mexican *bracero* workers came to work in the fields during World War II, the U.S. Border Patrol began to use the term "illegal alien" to refer to Mexicans crossing over the border without legal permission (Nevins, 2002; Ngai, 2004; Reimers, 1998). Because so many Mexicans had been living in the United States when a significant portion of the West was a part of Mexico, and because so many workers had been brought to the U.S. to work, labeling Mexicans as "illegal aliens" construed all people of Mexican-origin as highly visible, easily identifiable law breakers (Nevins, 2002). In her book, *Impossible Subjects*, Ngai (2004) traces the development of the "illegal alien" concept in a compelling history of the negative reception of Latino and Asian immigrants in the United States.

As anti-immigration sentiment grew, laws were enacted to impose severe immigration quotas. Racial maps were drawn; in 1965, the Hart Cellar Act, created western hemisphere quotas, quotas that were established because of the influx of Mexican immigrants coming across the border (Ngai, 2004). The Hart Cellar Act regulated which types of immigrants were desirable (skilled, educated, white, etc.) and which were not (unskilled, illiterate and nonwhite).

History provides a convincing case that immigrant law has been defined by racial issues. Today, the current immigration debate is about the large segment of immigrants who have come into the country illegally (this group is largely Mexican) and whether such "illegal aliens" should be given a path to citizenship. While the Illegal Immigration Reform and Immigrant Responsibility Act (IIRRIRA) of 1996 bars undocumented immigrants from receiving many federal and state services, immigration scholars have argued for both more restrictive (Brimelow, 1995; Huntington, 2004) and more expansive opportunities (Motomura, 2006; Perry, 2006; Pickus, 2006) for the more than 11 million estimated undocumented immigrants living in the country. Part of the immigration debate raging in the United States today is the highly charged issue of whether or not undocumented high school students should have access to in-state tuition (Godson, 2005; Jimenez, Zarate, & Wiggins, 2005; National Conference on State Legislatures, 2005; Stancill, 2005; United States General Accounting Office, 2004).

While the history of immigration law describes how immigrants have been discriminated against because of their race (Ngai, 2004), and how immigration law has privileged white immigrants (Nevins, 2002), there remains a gap in the literature regarding undocumented high school immigrants and their experiences in the higher education system.   Courts have challenged the in-state tuition laws for undocumented immigrants (Day, 2005), and universities have had to pay fines for admitting and financing --with federal dollars-- undocumented students at their campuses (Jordan, 2006).

LATINO STUDENTS IN EDUCATION

The history of immigration law traces difficulties that immigrants of color have faced historically. The American education system echoes this difficult process for students of color. While any child regardless of their immigration status is granted access to K-12 public education, the U.S. education system historically has practiced educational inequities that began with the prohibition of African-American students (Anderson, 1988) and continues today through the varied education inequities practiced upon students of color.

Lack of access to fair and quality education for Latinos has been well documented over time (Donato, 1996; Donato, 1997; Gonzalez, 1990; San Miguel, 1987). Latinos are the fastest growing minority population in the United States totaling nearly 14 percent of the U.S. population in 2007 alone (Kohler & Lazarin, 2007). By 2008, nearly one in six U.S. residents was Hispanic (U.S. Census, 2009). Yet at the same time Hispanic graduation rates from high school (about 53 percent) (Orfield et al. 2004) and transition into college, less than 10% of Latinos age 25-29 earn a bachelor's degree, are not keeping pace with the population's growth in the United States (Pew Hispanic Center, 2007).

Latino immigrant students account for more than half of the immigrant youth population in the United States, and drop-out rates for foreign-born Latino students constitute nearly 25 percent of all dropouts in the United States (Kohler & Lazarin, 2007). Fostering the educational disparities toward Latino youth, they more often attend low-income schools, are less likely to be enrolled in AP math and science coursework, and attend schools that offer fewer rigorous courses than their white peers. The so-called "leaking pipeline" in education reveals that of 100 Latino children who begin school together, only 50 will graduate from high school, and only 10 of those will complete a college degree (Solórzano et al., 2005). While 84 percent of non-Latino whites who are 18 years or older will attend college, only about 46 percent of Mexican-American students attend any type of college. More than 50 percent of all Latino students begin in community college, a route that significantly decreases the possibility of completing their education (Solórzano et al., 2005). As the Latino community grows at record pace in relation to its non-Latino white, and African American counterparts, demographers do not predict any measurable degree of parity in future access to education (Murdock, 2006).

During the K-12 experience, research has shown that Latinos often have been relegated to separate, unequal, and inferior public schools (Garcia, 2001; Gonzalez, 1990). In *Subtractive Schooling*, Angela Valenzuela (1999) demonstrated how school systems in Houston practiced subtractive schooling. Mexican-American students and recent immigrants often rejected the process of schooling because schools did not elicit an authentic sense of caring toward them or toward their education. Valenzuela demonstrated that school was trying to subtract students' Latino culture from them and to replace that with a culture that viewed the Latino culture and community as worthless.

Valenzuela and other researchers (Conchas, 2006; Gonzalez et al., 2003) have demonstrated how schools and counselors have tracked Latino students into non-academic curriculum paths. Gilberto Conchas (2006) showed how tracking reflects both class relations and racial stratification. In these tracks, kids are under-motivated and rarely encouraged to consider college as a future opportunity. Research has verified that English-as-Second-Language (ESL) classes rarely provided discussions about college (Gonzalez et al., 2003; Oliverez, 2005a; Oliverez, 2005b). Removing students from non-academic tracks is important. Research on college prep programs such as AVID demonstrates that these programs have succeeded in placing every student in a "college track" curriculum (Moll & Ruiz, 2002).

Other research on Latinos in education shows that schools practice "deficit thinking"[5] about the abilities of their Latino students (Villenas, 1996). Attempting to counter such deficit-thinking, research has been conducted on how teachers can use what their Latino students bring with them from their home communities in order to teach them. The term "Funds of Knowledge" was coined to help describe the many strengths and talents that Latino students bring with them from their often working-class and immigrant backgrounds (Moll et al., 1992; Gonzalez et al. 2005). There also is a wealth of research that describes how bilingualism is an asset for children from homes where English is not their first language (Cummins, 1980; Cummins, 1986; Cummins, 1995). Gary Orfield comments that bilingualism, rather than being a detriment to integrating into U.S. society, is a key factor for preserving the future prospects of Latino students (Suárez-Orozco & Paez, 2002).

In *Legacies* (2001), Portes and Rumbaut utilize survey data to demonstrate how different types of acculturation and incorporation into U.S. society affect Latino children's schooling experiences. Portes and Rumbaut describe three models of acculturation. In "dissonant acculturation," children assimilate into mainstream culture quickly, often causing problems in their relationship with their parents, who have not assimilated as quickly. In "consonant acculturation," the learning process of assimilation is more gradual and the home language is often abandoned after one generation. In "selective acculturation," children maintain their ethnic identity and are embedded in a positive co-ethnic community that fuses their immigrant identity with their American identity. In the selective acculturation model, children have the most positive schooling and home experiences. Portes and Rumbaut also use data from the "Mexican-case" to demonstrate how negative incorporation into a country can create social and economic inferiority that cannot be overcome without attaining high levels of education.

The "Mexican Case" in Portes and Rumbaut's acculturation model (2001) emphasizes what an important role negative racial constructions play in migration to the United States. These hegemonic and pervasive negative racial constructions toward Latinos may also contribute to their retaining ties to their home countries (Goldring, 1998). These ties may provide relief from the negative stereotypes and negative social

---

[5] Deficit thinking involves teachers and school officials believing that students have deficiencies, because of their personal backgrounds, that would keep them from being successful at school.

mirroring (Suárez-Orozco & Suárez-Orozco, 2001) that occurs when Mexicans migrate to the United States.

Other research describes why Latino students often have such a difficult time accessing opportunities for higher education. Studies on cultural and social capital display how mainstream school rewards the culture of the dominant middle class (Bourdieu, 1986; Horvat, Weininger, & Lareau, 2003; Lareau, 2000). Social capital can be defined as the, "aggregate or potential resources which are linked to possession of a durable network of more or less institutionalized relationships of mutual acquaintance and recognition—in other words, to members in a group—which provides its members with the banking of collectively own capital, a "credential" which entitles them to credit in the various senses of the word." (Bourdieu, 1986, p.242) Children outside the mainstream culture often have difficulty accessing social networks to help them learn about the college application process (K. Gonzalez et al., 2003; Stanton-Salazar & Spina, 2003; Stanton-Salazar & Spina, 2000). In many cases, schools reward only the capital of whitestream (Grande, 2000) knowledge (Carreon et al., 2005; Perna & Titus, 2005), which leaves students from non-white backgrounds at a severe disadvantage.

For many Latino students, particularly those who are first-generation or from recent immigrant households, the nuclear family does not possess cultural capital regarding the college process. Therefore, they must rely on institutional agents to give them access to social capital networks that will provide them access to college information (Stanton-Salazar, 1995; Stanton-Salazar & Spina, 2000; Stanton-Salazar & Spina, 2003). Research also has demonstrated that Latino students feel constrained by institutional neglect, are provided insufficient knowledge about and given limited opportunities for attending college (K.Gonzalez et al., 2003). Susan Auerbach (2002) has shown how Latino parents who attempted to participate in their child's education faced struggles of bureaucratic rebuff and memories of their own negative experiences in the system when attempting to help their child.

LATINO STUDENTS IN HIGHER EDUCATION

Despite such struggles, Latino students have increasingly accessed the college pipeline. Latinos compose about 18 percent of the total college-age population and represent about 10.4 percent of the college-going population (Kohler & Lazarin, 2007).

The little research that has been conducted on high-achieving Latino students indicates that students who have successfully continued into higher education did so with the support of their families and of individual persons in the school system that created bridges to information (Conchas, 2001, Gandara, 2006; Gandara, 1995; Lopez, 2004; Stanton-Salazar & Spina, 2000). Nevertheless, many Latino families have created a "culture of possibility" for their children by modeling a rigorous work ethic and choosing to provide the best education possible for their child (Gandara, 1995; Valdes, 1996).

The research on high achieving students, Latinos in particular, shows that in spite of the low overall performance of Latino high school students, many of them defy the odds and succeed in school (Conchas, 2001; Conchas & Clark, 2002; Gandara, 1997, Gibson, 1997, Mehan et al. 1996). Recently, Gilberto Conchas (2006) and Prudence Carter (2005) explored how factors regarding race affect high-achieving students. Building on the work of Gandara (1995), Conchas's book *The Color of Success: Race and High-Achieving Urban Youth* (2006), explores how some low-income students from racial minority backgrounds succeed despite the inequality in the urban school environment. By implication, his research demonstrates the importance of "social scaffolds" within special honors academies and course tracks to foster a culture of academic success for Latino students. His findings identified structures in the public schools that create both success and failure for Latino students.

Prudence Carter (2005) showed how success in school is deeply shaped by feelings of inclusiveness in the school setting and explored how different minority students navigate this terrain. In "'*Keepin it real': School Success Beyond Black and White*," Carter examined how students' perceptions of themselves are linked to their racial, ethnic, cultural and gendered ideologies. She described three categories of students within the school setting she observed.

> 1) The "noncompliant believers" understood what cultural behaviors in the school led to academic success but chose to exert little effort to conform to those behaviors to resist the dominant (white) culture in the school.
> 2) The "cultural mainstreamers" accepted the cultural behaviors as correct and assimilated into the mainstream in an effort to shed their ethnic and cultural identity and to fit more easily into the system.

3) The "cultural straddlers" were able to have bicultural perspectives, simultaneously understanding the school rules and codes but also remaining connected with their co-ethnic peers.

Research by Carter (2005) and Conchas (2006) discusses the complexity of being a high-achieving student of color and of the negotiations which occur inside the classrooms.

Rarely does the existing literature flesh out the differences in Latino generational and citizenship experiences. The experiences of a fifth generation Chicano student is significantly different from that of an immigrant student whose crossed the border a little over a month before. The differences in existing educational levels of immigrant students (Massey, Durand, & Malone, 2002) and their status as U.S. citizens or undocumented immigrants greatly affect their chances for success and incorporation into U.S. society (Portes & Rumbaut, 2001).

IMMIGRANT LATINO STUDENTS

The Latino immigrant experience in the United States could be categorized, at best, as an ambivalent reception to them as human bodies that comprise the low-wage work force the U.S. relies upon to fill jobs that native workers will not accept (Murillo, 2002; Rivera, 1997; Suárez-Orozco & Paez, 2002). Children from immigrant families are often viewed with deficit thinking because they come to school lacking the middle class cultural capital needed for success in the public school system (Horvat et al., 2003; Lareau, 2000).

Scholars Marcela Suárez-Orozco and Carola Suárez-Orozco have dedicated their lives to researching and understanding the experiences of immigrant students (2001a; 2001b; 2002; 2005). Utilizing ethnographic methods to illuminate statistics, these authors have identified why immigrants come to the United States, how they are accepted by mainstream society, what the role of immigrants is in U.S. society, and what psychological factors are faced by immigrant children and children with immigrant parents. Among the obstacles faced by immigrant students, the authors describe the factors of acculturation, language acquisition, the affects of social mirroring and economic and neighborhood characteristics of the places they live in the United States.

One of the more important psychological factors Suárez-Orozco and Suárez-Orozco (2001) found is the cultural "frame of separation" that occurs when a child and parent are separated from each other (parents often come to the United States before their children and send for them later once they are established), and the transition that occurs when children are reunited with their parents in the United States. The authors affirm the difficulty to both child and parents of the acculturation process (learning the rules of a new society and how they fit into that society), and the problems that often occur when immigrant children are more exposed to American culture than their parents through schooling. One part of the transition process the authors highlight is the uncomfortable position many students are put in when they become translators for their parents, and are responsible for private information that they would not have otherwise have become privy to. Suárez-Orozco and Suárez-Orozco (2001) also stress the process of social mirroring in which children --as the recipients of negative attitudes-- may come to internalize the prejudices that the dominant society holds about particular (most commonly Mexican) immigrant groups. Negative stereotypes about Mexicans being lazy, stupid, and prone to crime are displayed to the immigrant students in and out of school (Cornelius, 2004; Fergus, 2002; Murillo, 2002). The authors argue that people are dependent on reflections of themselves and come to internalize the feelings that the outside community has towards them. For immigrant school children, the consequences of social mirroring may include self-defeating behaviors like misbehaving in school, not doing well because of low expectations, and, in the most extreme circumstances, joining gangs or dropping out of school altogether. While not all immigrant children internalize the negative social mirroring about the Mexican immigrant community, the danger of this is extremely high for this group of students.

In *Transnational Factors and School Success of Mexican Immigrants,* Regina Cortina (Cortina & Gendreau, 2003) notes that teachers are often influenced by the cultural deficit perspectives about the value that Mexican families place on education. Cortina warns that educators need to understand the various aspects of the cultural background: 1) These children arrive with many needs, not only in education but also in health, nutritional and living standards 2) Some children may lack literacy skills in Spanish, and their parents may have little to no understanding of the culture of American schools, 3) "Myth of Return Phenomena" may keep parents attached to past customs and less willing to assimilate into new American culture (73). Ultimately, Cortina argues that teachers must learn and appreciate the cultural background of Mexican children in order to help foster in them self-respect for their academic and cultural identities.

In *Made in American: Immigrant Students in our Public Schools*, Laurie Olsen (1997) describes how the public school system forces immigrant students to socialize themselves within racial categories and to choose which "race track" they will identify with once they arrived in the U.S. Arriving from countries where race is not seen along such a rigid black-white continuum, many immigrant students feel that they do not belong anywhere in the new school system. Olsen also describes how children are often disappointed that learning English or doing well in school is not a ticket for acceptance because of the racialized categories into which they are placed in the school system.

Carola Suárez-Orozco (1989) has shown that immigrant students use a "dual frame of reference" to navigate successfully within the school system. This dual frame allows them to reflect on the difficulties they would be facing if they were still in their country of origin (political unrest, economic instability, etc.) and then use those references to develop positive attitudes and academic identity in the States. Research suggests that this "dual frame of reference" is one reason why first-generation immigrants are more successful than their second-generation counterparts (Valenzuela, 1999). Some scholars (Conchas, 2006; Gibson et al., 2004) argue that it is possible for immigrant students to develop identities that help them practice "accommodation without assimilation" (Gibson, 1988).

Other scholars contend that school is yet another location or space where immigrant students are subordinated and viewed as a "problem" within their community (DuBois, 1993; Murillo, 2002; Wortham et al., 2002). Research on the new Latino diaspora to the South in the U.S. identifies difficulties faced by recent Latino immigrants. Enrique Murillo (2002) demonstrated that immigrants in North Carolina were "disciplined" and forced to adhere to societal norms. Murillo argues that school experiences of Mexican immigrants mirror the poor work experiences of Mexicans in general. He also showed that, even while immigrant parents try to get a good education for their children, these parents have difficulty because they are viewed by the community as less deserving.

UNDOCUMENTED IMMIGRANT STUDENTS AND HIGHER EDUCATION

The Pew Hispanic Center (2008) estimates that there are approximately 11.9 million undocumented immigrants living in the United States. Of these 11.9 million, nearly 9.6 have come to the U.S. from Latin

America, with Mexico representing nearly 7 million of those immigrants. In 2009 the College Board estimated that nearly 1.8 million of these 11.9 million undocumented immigrants were children under the age of 18, up from 1.6 million in 2004 (Urban Institute, 2004). It is not surprising given the make-up of undocumented immigrants in the United States, that having undocumented status suggests that those same students are highly likely to be of Latino origin and low-socioeconomic status (Erisman & Looney, 2007).

While research on immigrant students has become more prevalent, literature specifically regarding undocumented high school and college students is limited. In 2005 the Bell Policy Center (Protopsaltis, 2005) released a report outlining in-state tuition policies for undocumented students in each of the 10 states that allow access to in-state rates. This report noted that while one in 20 undocumented high school students may attend some type of college, they will then face the hurdle of finding gainful employment even if they completed college. For this reason, the report endorsed the DREAM Act, which would allow undocumented students in-state tuition and a path toward citizenship. The Bell Policy Center as well as hundreds of national organizations (College Board, the Hispanic Association of Colleges and Universities, National Immigration Law Center, National Council of La Raza) sees this approach as the solution that undocumented student advocates should promote for both federal and state levels.[6] During the 2006 legislative year, the federal DREAM Act bill sat attached to an immigration reform bill that was never heard or voted on during the entire congressional session. A version of the bill was debated in 2007, but failed to garner enough votes in the US Senate.

In *Children of Immigration*, Suárez-Orozco and Suárez-Orozco (2001) remark that, "The legal status of an immigrant child influences, perhaps more so than national origins, his or her experiences and life chances."(33) In their research, the authors explored the psychological repercussions of a child's legal status, including feelings of being "hunted," having distrust and fear in the school setting, and feeling a horrible sense of injustice once they discover they will not likely be able to go beyond high school. These scholars identified the anger, hopelessness, and depression that may occur among undocumented high school students. Ultimately, the authors argue, "While some have

---

[6] For a full list of national organizations that endorse the DREAM Act please see http://democracyinaction.org/dia/organizations/NILC/images/DREAM%20Endorsers.htm

worried about the costs incurred by taxpayers in educating undocumented immigrant children, the long term costs of not educating them are even greater." (35)

In California, Luis Urrieta (Urrieta et al., 2003) gathered personal *testimonios* from immigrant students. In these *testimonios,* Urrieta (2003) demonstrated that undocumented high school students succeed in high school despite, rather than because of, the public school system they navigated each day. Paz Oliverez (2005a, 2005b) conducted qualitative interviews of California undocumented high school students. Despite HB 540 (passed in 2001), which allows undocumented high school students who have attended a California high school to be eligible for in-state tuition and state-sponsored aid, Oliverez notes how few undocumented students take advantage of these opportunities. Her research revealed that students are unfamiliar with the opportunity to attend college because they are not viewed as "college material" and often are unaware that an in-state tuition policy exists. Oliverez documents the difficulty of applying to college and navigating the financial aid process for an undocumented student. As an outgrowth of her research, Oliverez (Oliverez et al. 2006) created a manual that helps undocumented students understand their rights and the laws that allow undocumented students in California to access in-state tuition. This document provides invaluable information for California students who are the first in their family to navigate the college application process.

Research on highly talented undocumented students in California reveals the talent and abilities which are lost by not allowing more undocumented students to access the higher education system (Perez, 2006; Perez et al. 2009). This research revealed the personal resiliency and the strong work ethic undocumented students displayed throughout their K-12 experiences. Research on these same students also examined undocumented college students in community college, and identified the sacrifices that they make to attend university despite their undocumented status (Cortes, 2008).

In Texas, Silvia DeLeon (2005) and Teri Albrecht (2007) completed qualitative research on undocumented high school students who were attending one of several public universities. In Texas, undocumented students who have attended a Texas high school may also be granted in-state tuition and access to state aid. DeLeon described how undocumented immigrant student's resiliency facilitated their successful transition from high school to college. Her research examined the "ambiguous loss" felt by undocumented immigrants (feelings that they may never be able to return to their country of origin, and may also never feel completely at home in the United States) and showed they were able to rebound successfully despite exposure to great risks and obstacles in their lives. This resiliency gave them an advantage when coping with adversity by persevering in the face of great obstacles. Albrecht's research (2007) highlighted the lack of services for undocumented students' specific needs and the pressures of their legal status including pressure to be a role model for other students in the same position.

Stella Flores' body of research (Flores, forthcoming 2010, Flores & Chapa, 2009, Flores & Horn, 2009) examines the effects of in-state tuition policies and financial aid on undocumented students. Her quantitative results show that undocumented students living in states that have in-state policies (10 including Texas, California, and New York) are more likely to attend college than students who live in states without such a policy. In addition, her research at the University of Texas Austin demonstrates that undocumented students at that institution are remaining in college at same rates as their Latino peers who are US citizens and legal residents. Her research provides a compelling argument that if give an opportunity, students will take advantage of the in-state tuition policy and will work hard to "improve their human capital potential (Flores & Chapa, 2006, p. 106)."

In New York, Ruben Barato (2009) explored how urban community colleges in states with in-state tuition policies serve undocumented students. Existing research shows that community colleges have given the least resistance and the most financial access to higher education (Rangel, 2001). Community colleges were less likely to prevent admission because students lack the proper legal documents (Dozier, 1992; Dozier, 1995; Dozier, 2001). Building on previous research, Barato's research affirmed that the urban community college was a nurturing and positive experience for the student's in his study. Barato's research also highlighted the education resilience and perseverance of undocumented students who attended community college.

Andre Perry (2006) did a case study on undocumented immigrants and U.S. political figures conceptualizations of membership in a democratic society. He examined peoples' attitudes toward Texas House Bill 1403 which grants in-state tuition to undocumented immigrants. His study set residency, social awareness, reciprocation, investment, identification, patriotism, destiny, and law abidingness as the basis of a framework he named *substantive membership*. Given his findings on a shared understanding of membership, Perry argued that undocumented immigrants who have become substantive members in U.S. society should receive financial aid.

In addition, immigration lawyer and higher education professor Dr. Michael Olivas (Olivas, 1995; Olivas, 2002; Olivas, 2004; Olivas, 2005; Olivas, 2008; Olivas, 2009) has studied history of immigration law over the last twenty years, including *Plyer v. Doe* (1982) and college residency requirements. Dr. Olivas' work highlights the conflicting policies and laws of college residency requirement as they pertain to undocumented high school students. Dr. Olivas (Olivas, 2002; Olivas, 2004) has argued that in-state tuition policies are viable options because in-state residency is a benefit entirely determined by state, rather than federal government. He also contends that provisions of the IRIRA do not prohibit states from enacting residency statutes for undocumented students, and that the literal wording inside in-state residency bills can be inclusive of undocumented students. Ultimately, Olivas argues that states have the jurisdiction to make their own policies regarding in-state tuition policies without fear of legal repercussions from the federal government.

The Transnational Student Experience
Since all the students involved in this research were born in Mexico and migrated to the United States after the age of seven (and most at the age of 11), their experiences comprise the "transnational experience." While some research focuses on the types of transnational experience a person encounters including "transnational sojourners" (Hamann & Zuniga, 2006), those immigrants who may return to their country origin, or the idea of "transnational from below" (Smith and Guarnizo, 1998), which defines the decision to leave one's country of origin because of economic constraints placed upon them, this research aligns best with studies that explore the identities and characteristics of those who lived the transcultural experience. The transcultural experience includes both those students who have been able to return to their country of origin and students who maintain their Mexican identity yet have been unable, in the majority of cases, to return to their country of birth.

Suárez-Orozco and Suárez-Orozco (2001) describe a conceptual framework much like Portes and Rumbaut's (1999) theories of accommodation and assimilation, wherein most students choose one of three paths.   At one end, students practice ethnic flights by disassociating themselves from their ethnic community, and at the opposite end are students who develop completely resistant norms to the dominant group.   In the middle, where the researchers argue most students remain, students struggle to maintain links with their own ethnic group as well as dominant population.   Suárez-Orozco and Suárez-Orozco refer to this process as transculturation, where "individuals create hybrid identities and cultural transformations." (121)

Jocelyn Solis (Solis, 2001; Solis, 2003; Solis, 2004; Solis, 2005), who examined undocumented immigrants involved in an advocacy group in New York City, faults the majority of transnational studies for focusing on changes to local practices in the general community rather than on the individual lives of the transnational students.   Patricia Sanchez (2001) suggests that such "lived transnationalism" involves being part of multiple communities and requires multiple negotiations and shifts, and argues that more attention should be given to how their transnational identity shapes how immigrant students negotiate their lives inside and outside school.

Throughout the literature on transnationalism, scholars argue that immigration today is no longer a one-way process because over time, "migrant communities become culturally transnationalized incorporating ideologies, practices, expectations, and political claims from both societies to create a culture of migration that is distinct from the culture of both the sending and receiving nation." (Massey, Goldring and Durand, 2002, p.1501) Research by Susan Dicker (2006) shows that within the transnational experience, ties to the homeland are not cut off even after a second generation may be born in the U.S. Ultimately, others argue, transnational students are some of the most adaptive persons in this era of globalism (Trueba, 2002; Trueba, 2004). Enrique Trueba's writing highlights the strengths of the transnational student (Trueba & Bartolome, 2000; Trueba, 2002; Trueba, 2004). For Trueba, the transnational student differed from the immigrant student in small but important ways. For Trueba, the transnational student was immersed in the culture of origin (sometimes physically back and forth), as well as in their American lifestyle. The transnational student returned to their country of origin (not always in a physical sense) by their understanding of their home country's current events, the maintenance of heritage language, and their refusal to assimilate completely into the American mainstream culture.

Trueba observed that transnational students have a unique capacity to live in different cultures, to master multiple languages and to navigate multiple roles and relationships in American society. His research highlighted the strengths of the transnational student including their knowledge and fluency in both English and Spanish, and their full participation in both American and Mexican culture. Trueba wrote about transnational students' strong sense of ethnic affiliation and the strong ties they kept with their families and their culture from their country of origin. Trueba argued that transnational students possess cultural capital that will soon be viewed as a cultural commodity. He argued that their consistent ability to redefine themselves and to act as "border crossers" (Anzaldua, 1987), would some day put them ahead of their American counterparts. While transnational students who crossed between Texas and Mexico were Trueba's utopian vision of the transnational student, his writings indicate that being a transnational student has more to do with the mental crossings that transnational students are able to navigate.

POLICY REPORTS AND RESEARCH IN NORTH CAROLINA

North Carolina has one of the fastest growing Latino populations in the United States from approximately 76,000 Latinos in North Carolina in 1990 to well over 600,000 by 2007 (Pew Hispanic Center, 2007; U.S. Census, 2009). The Pew Hispanic Center (2009) estimates that the majority of Latinos in North Carolina are not U.S. citizens.

Latino immigration into North Carolina has occurred for numerous reasons, including changes in immigration policy after 9/11, changes and restructuring of the U.S. economy in relation to globalization, and the formation of economic and social networks (Vasquez, Seales, & Marquardt, 2006). A robust economy in North Carolina and the opportunity for work created a need for low-wage workers, who were often recruited by North Carolina companies (Kandel & Parrado, 2004; Krissman, 2000). Job opportunities in towns which offered inexpensive housing and a safe place to raise a family away from crimes were attractive incentives to Latino immigrants coming into the United States.

In *New Latino Destinations*, authors Vasquez, Seales and Marquardt (2006) note that "although there are some highly-skilled industrial workers from Latin American, the great majority of Latinos have been integrated into this flexible unskilled labor pool." (17) With a robust economy that continues to grow steadily, North Carolina has established itself as a new immigrant gateway. With the arrival of new immigrants come challenges including the issue of undocumented immigration.

In 2006 the University of North Carolina Business School released a report on the nine-billion-dollar impact of the Hispanic population on the state's economy (Kasarda & Johnson, 2006). The report also showed the great impact Latino students had on the public education system. From the school year 2000-2001 through 2004-2005, Latino students accounted for 57 percent of the growth in public schools statewide. North Carolina education systems' LEP enrollment in North Carolina has risen 327 percent between 1995-2005, and this rise in enrollment is largely a result of new foreign and American-born Latino students (Kohler & Lazarin, 2007). Kasarda & Johnson (2006) suggest that the growth of both Latino U.S. citizens and undocumented immigrants will continue for the next 50 years.

The New Latino South and the Challenge to Public Education (Tomas Rivera Policy Institute, 2005), highlights the challenges for new immigrant communities in the South: the lack of resources invested in educating immigrant students, the underrepresentation of Latino high school students on college campuses in the South, and the lack of teacher training opportunities to help schools have qualified teachers. This report called for more research and advocated that undocumented immigrant students have access to in-state tuition at public universities.

However, specific research on Latino high school students in North Carolina's education system has been relatively limited. Valencia and Johnson (2006) conducted a survey of high school students at a leadership conference conducted by the North Carolina Society for Hispanic Professionals (NCSHP), in which the participants reported few perceived barriers at school. Among the barriers that were the most prevalent were discrimination (8%), school program attendance (8%), and lack of time for parental involvement (8%). While 92 percent of the students claimed high levels of personal parental support, their parents' lack of involvement in school came from work schedules, lack of English, and unfamiliarity with American school systems. Students in this survey with high levels of acculturation (defined by English language preference and a large number of years in the U.S.) had a greater desire to attend college than students with low acculturation levels. Interestingly enough, those students with low acculturation levels (defined by fewer years in the United States, and filling out the survey in Spanish) had higher aspirations for doing well in school and in having a good career after high school than their highly-acculturated peers. This contradiction may reflect the high-achieving desires of recent immigrants, who may be unfamiliar with the importance of college in the United States, but who clearly value hard work and providing for themselves and their families.

The review of the literature reveals that Latinos often negotiate inequitable educational opportunities and that access to higher education for Latino students, in particular to recent immigrants, has been shaped by immigration policy, lack of social networks, and negative social reception in both the K-12 and higher education systems. The research reiterates that accessing the college pipeline for students who are not U.S. citizens is extremely difficult.

CHAPTER 3

Critical Race Theory and Latino Critical Theory

Because the issue of undocumented students accessing higher education is framed by issues of race[7] and ethnicity, theories that highlight the centrality of race in American society can be applied. I have utilized Critical Race Theory (CRT) and Latino Critical Theory (LatCrit) to interpret and critique the experiences of the undocumented Mexican immigrant students who are denied access to higher education in North Carolina.

CRITICAL RACE THEORY

CRT built upon, and extended, critical legal studies (CLS), which was created by legal scholars who were generally dissatisfied with the classic tenets of general legal thought, and with the lack of recognition of social forces on legal change (Crenshaw, et al. 1995; Delgado, 1995; Delgado & Stefanic, 1998, Delgado & Stefanic, 2001; Ladson-Billings & Tate; Williams, 1995; Tate, 1997, Villenas & Deyhle, 1999). CLS (Tate, 1997) argues that 1) past legal doctrine privileged a white perspective of society and because of this had numerous contradictions and 2) civil

---

[7] While race is ultimately a social construction, I understand it to be real in its everyday consequences.

rights laws need to include a critical analysis of racialized issues in the United States (Tate, 1997). Although, CLS developed from the social theories of Carl Marx and Max Weber, whose modes of political analysis combined functionalist methods with radical goals, CRT determined that CLS was not focusing enough on the hegemonic role of racism.

CRT has consistently challenged the inferiority paradigm of people of color, which characterizes people of color as less capable and less worthy than the dominant white majority in US society. This inferiority paradigm was socially constructed over time, partially because of legal doctrine, and has come to be accepted as the standard or norm (Haney Lopez, 1996). In challenging the inferiority paradigm, CRT also emphasizes how U.S. society privileges the Eurocentric perspective. This Eurocentric perspective is one which, "adheres to a Eurocentric perspective founded on covert and overt assumptions regarding white superiority, territorial expansion and 'American' democratic ideals such as meritocracy, objectivity, and individuality." (Delgado-Bernal, 2002, p.11) CRT also argues that the Eurocentric perspective and the system of white privilege (McIntosh, 1997) shapes belief systems and social practices in everyday life, including the policies and practices that occur in education systems nationwide.

Solórzano, Villapando, and Oseguera (2005) summarize five key components of CRT:

> 1) The centrality of race and racism.[8] At the most basic level, race and racism are, "deeply engrained through historical consciousness and ideological choices about race, which in turn has deeply shaped the U.S. legal system and the ways people think about law, racial categories and privilege." (Parker & Lynn, 2002, p.9) Race is endemic and literally the "air we breathe" in the United States.

---

[8] For the purpose of this study racism is defined as the "belief in the inherent superiority of one race over all others thereby the right to dominance." (Lorde, 1992. p. 496) Manning Marable extends this definition by declaring that racism is a "system of ignorance, exploitation, and power used to oppress African-Americans, Latinos Asians, Pacific Americans, American Indians and other people on the basis of ethnicity, culture, mannerisms and color." (Marable, 1992, p.5). Marable's definition is important because it shifts discourse on race from black and white to include multiple communities of color and their varied experiences (Solórzano and Yosso, 2002).

2) The need to challenge the dominant ideology. This ideology claims neutrality and endorses the myth of meritocracy and of equal opportunity in this country. In higher education, the myth of color blindness or race neutrality in admission practices, meritocratic testing practices, and the myth of equal opportunity for all students should be challenged.

3) A commitment to social justice and praxis. This commitment underlies the work of CRT scholars and attempts to align theory and practice together in their work.

4) The importance of voice and the centrality of the lived experiences of people of color. This tenet validates the importance of narrative and the representation of voices that exist "on the margins." The experiential knowledge of people of color must be recognized and validated as legitimate ways of knowing.

5) The interdisciplinary nature of CRT's attention to history and context. Historical context reveals the use of "race, ethnicity, national origin, language, class and the changing conception of justice in the construction and implementation of laws that influence higher education." (Solórzano, Villapando & Oseguera, 2005, p.275)

These five tenets are utilized throughout this research. The centrality of race and racism (Ladson-Billings & Tate, 1995) is central to the policies and laws that bar undocumented students from accessing in-state tuition. CRT's challenge to the dominant ideology (Bell, 2005; Brayboy, 2004), parallel the tactics and strategies the students and teachers used as they navigated the college application process. False claims of ideological neutrality (Harris, 1993; Solórzano et al., 2005) are reflected in the public education systems' empty promises made to academically qualified students. My own work as director of the Latino Outreach and the work of my teacher-ally participants demonstrate a commitment to both social justice and praxis. The importance of voice (Delgado-Bernal, 2002; Hill Collins, 1999) justifies the individual stories of the student participants about their journeys across borders (both physical and metaphorical). Finally, an attempt to unite qualitative ethnography with immigration law and policy through an interdisciplinary perspective will focus on the importance of history and context to the undocumented students in North Carolina.

CRT also calls for a change in educational research to examine the historical and legal background of the United States, the ideology of racism in the country, the influence and treatment of minority communities, and the prevailing views of students of color in educational studies. CRT scholars have looked carefully at structures, practices and policies and the ways in which they create and perpetuate racial and ethnic inequalities in the United States. In educational research's seminal CRT manifesto, *Toward a Critical Race Theory of Education*, authors Gloria Ladson-Billings and William F. Tate (1995) argue that past theories related to academic inequalities among different groups of students have rested on foundations of gender and class. The authors argue for a more careful examine of race within critical theory to explore racial educational disparities.

Ladson-Billings and Tate (1995) identify three propositions supporting race-based inquiries in education: 1) Race continues to be a significant factor in determining inequity in the United States. While multiple classifications and categories exist in both the scientific and social world, the notion of race is still commonly used to explain differences in economic and social classes. 2) U.S. society is based on property rights, synonymous with power throughout American history. Because African Americans were considered the "property" of white plantation owners, there was no call to secure their human rights; thus slavery became justified. This legacy of slavery and its connection to property rights has created a paradigm wherein individuals with better property (i.e. more wealth) are entitled to better schools, and those with less property are forced into inferior schooling. 3) The intersection of race and property creates an analytic tool through which we can understand social inequities in school such as the desegregation of public schools, the increase of "white flight" because of that desegregation, and the benefits afforded to white students as a result of desegregation (i.e. model school integration programs are judged as successful when white students have not left the system). By carefully focusing on these propositions and by honoring the knowledge and voice of people of color affected by these social values, Ladson-Billings and Tate (1995) argued that CRT has the potential to remedy disparities within the American educational system.

The tenets of CRT and the propositions of Ladson-Billings and Tate (1995) frame this research. It is also important to acknowledge that for people of color the salience of race is only one of the many categories that influences how people are subordinated, and that different socio-cultural factors affect and intersect with one another (Crenshaw, 1993).

Several important supplementary concepts shaped the data analysis: double-consciousness (DuBois, 1993); structural determinism (Delgado & Stefanic, 2001); convergence theory (Bell, 1979; Bell, 2005); and the importance of voice (Bell, 2005; Olivas, 1990; Delgado-Bernal, 2002).

Double-Consciousness

W.E.B. DuBois (1993) describes the notion double-consciousness as African-Americans' ability to have more critical insight into the world because of their precarious position in it. Ladson-Billings and Tate (1995) describe this ability as seeing the world through the eyes of one's oppressor as well through one's own eyes. This insight gives people of color a heightened sense of the world and the ability to see the world through multiple perspectives. It could be argued that Enrique Trueba (Trueba, 2002; Trueba, 2004) modified DuBois's argument to include the transnational community.

Structural Determinism

Working from a standpoint that undocumented students do possess strengths and should be valued for their bicultural and bilingual capital, the concept of structural determinism (Delgado, 1995; Tate, 1997) helps explain how current legal barriers prevent undocumented students from moving beyond a 12th grade education. While *Plyer v. Doe* (1982) grants access to the K-12 education system (although access and equity are entirely separate issues), the current legal system does not help transnational students to move beyond this point. Resistance to passing legislation such as the DREAM Act maintains the status quo. The current "illegality" argument needs be reconceptualized to allow undocumented students access to higher education.

The laws that currently exist in the majority of states (including South Carolina which explicitly prohibits undocumented students from attending college), maintain the status quo prohibiting undocumented students from in-state tuition. Interviews with teacher allies illuminated the nature of the structural determinism that prohibits them from helping their students pursue future academic options. Analysis of the allies' interviews shows that the current in-state tuition law in North Carolina affects the academic achievement of its undocumented students. These current laws also perpetuate second-class citizenship faced by the majority of the working-class Latinos in the Sunder Crossings community and in the state of North Carolina.

Delgado and Stefanic (1989) argue that innovative jurisprudence will likely come from those for whom the system has not worked. Undocumented students stand poised to be the innovators and creators of change in the legal system, a system whose categories have been prohibitive to this community in the past. CRT argues that those best ready to change such Draconian laws will be the students who have been harmed the most by them.

Convergence Theory
Convergence theory argues that the significant advancement for African Americans has only been achieved when the goals of blacks are consistent with the needs of whites. Thus policies regarding racial minorities have been and will only be supported when whites believe that they themselves have something to gain from changes (Bell, 1979; Bell, 1992; Bell, 2005).

For example, Derrick Bell argues that the Brown v. Board of Education decision (1954), which outlawed state supported school segregation, did not result from whites recognizing that current policies were wrong but from desegregation's making the white community look better in the eyes of the world. Bell found that while whites might support some civil rights legislation, they are not willing to support anything that might threaten their superior social status.

Convergence theory offers a possible explanation regarding why the general public in North Carolina is so strongly opposed to change in-state tuition policy and suggests what would be necessary to convince them otherwise. Convergence theory could also be used to examine whether economic, social, or moral arguments are the most persuasive when working with policymakers and the general public sentiment.

Voice
The importance of voice and the centrality of the "lived experiences" of people of color has been a cornerstone of critical race theory. Theorists argue that reality is socially constructed through the exchange of stories, and that those stories have often misrepresented people of color. By using voice and narrative as a framework for understanding, critical race theorists have accorded validity to the experiences of people of color, and placed communities of color into positions of power in both legal and educational discourse. Legal scholar S.L. Winter (1989) argues,

> In narrative we take experience and re-configure it in a
> conventional and comprehensible form. This is what gives

narratives its communicative power, and it is what makes a narrative a powerful tool of persuasion and therefore a potential transformative device for the empowered. (Winter as quoted in Tate, 1997, p.211)

Numerous scholars within both CRT and Latino Critical Theory have used narratives as a way to de-construct analysis of the law. CRT and LatCrit have developed the use of narrative by creating a type of hybridity in their texts that tacks between the world of policy and law and the experience of the everyday. Derrick Bell (Bell,1979; Bell, 1985; Bell, 1992), Richard Delgado (1995) and Mari Matsuda (1993), have demonstrated that story and counterstory supply the means to "name one's own reality." (Delgado & Stefanic, 1989)

Scholars have used stories in differing forms including personal stories or narratives, other people's stories and narratives, and composite stories. Personal stories (whether told from the point of the author, or told by the author about other people's experiences) typically recount people's experiences with various forms of racism, sexism and discrimination, and are juxtaposed with the analysis of the laws and policies that affect them. Critical race theorists thereby provide a larger social critique of the system. Created composite stories draw on multiple forms of data to examine the racialized experiences of people of color. Derrick Bell (2005) uses allegory as a method to discuss multiple forms of subordination. In his well-known "Civil Rights Chronicles" (1985), Bell creates a composite discourse that illuminates the false promises of civil rights law.

Richard Delgado's (Delgado & Stefanic, 1989; Delgado, 1995; Delgado & Stefanic, 2002) scholarship is devoted to exploring the role of story and counterstory in legal discourse. Delgado (1995) provides four arguments for the use of story and voice in academic scholarship:

1) Reality is socially constructed (primarily through one dominant voice)
2) Stories are powerful vehicles for changing people's ideas and mind sets
3) Stories can help build community among people
4) Stories provide members of marginalized groups with mental self-preservation.

Delgado's work has attempted to re-focus legal scholarship on particularities rather than "universal truths." These so-called "universal truths", accepted in American legal jurisprudence, follow the Anglo-American perspective rather than taking into account the contextual and historical conditions of people of color.

CRT identifies storytelling and giving voice to one's reality as important tools for achieving racial emancipation (Crenshaw, 1995; Delgado, 1995; Fernandez, 2002). The experiential knowledge of people of color is related through privileging forms of storytelling, family histories, oral histories, *testimonios* and narratives (Bell, 1985; Delgado, 1984; Olivas, 1990; Urrieta et al. 2003).   Privileging the voices of undocumented students in North Carolina, demonstrates that their *testimonios* are legitimate forms of resistance to oppression.

LATINO CRITICAL THEORY

While CRT, critiqued the more traditional civil rights model, Latino Critical Race Theory (LatCrit) has narrowed the focus to the historical experiences of Latinos in the United States and their particular subject position. In one of LatCrit's first articles in the Harvard Latino Law Review (1997) author Francisco Valdes argued that the "guideposts" of LatCrit are the foundational concepts of CRT, which include:

> (the) embrace of subjectivity, particularity, multiplicity, and intersectionality; the acceptance of legal scholarship's inevitable implication of power politics; the emphasis on praxis, social justice, reconstruction and transformation; the navigation of sameness and difference to build self-empowered communities; and the recognition of self critique's continuing importance to intellectual integrity. (57)

LatCrit with CRT shares many commitments that will help lead to more social equality, but, Valdes argues, "LatCrit at its best should operate as a close cousin, related to CRT in real and lasting ways, but not necessarily living under the same roof." (58)

While the central tenets of CRT help to illuminate all experiences of people of color, the purpose of CRT is not to essentialize experiences of subordination or to measure oppressions against each other. The Black communities struggle with slavery, civil rights, and desegregation are not the same issues as language politics or immigration, and scholars in both fields would not suggest that they should all be lumped together. Concepts within CRT such as intersectionality (Crenshaw, 1993) highlight multiple oppressions, including classism, racism, and nationalism, all which are issues relevant to undocumented Mexican students. The use of CRT is an umbrella of solidarity to show that people of color have multiple oppressions practiced upon them in different ways. Infusing CRT with a more detailed focus on LatCrit theory highlights the experiences of immigration while still focusing at a more general level on the salience of race.

LatCrit indeed differs from CRT in important and particular ways. Its development arose from the complex issues that were salient only to the Latino community but were not addressed by traditional CRT scholarship. These issues include, but are not limited to, immigration, language, and the conflict from diversity in the Latino community itself (from phenotype and language spoken, to citizenship status and class differences).

LatCrit theory addresses concerns relevant not only to the Latino community, but also to the "social and legal interests of Blacks, Asians, Native Americans, and other people of color who experience different yet similar forms of subordination under the nation's civil rights and immigration policy schemes." (Valdes, 1997, p.9) Just as civil rights issues affected not only the Black community, but also other persons of color experiencing inequitable conditions, research on immigration, language taught in school classrooms, and access to higher education for undocumented immigrants also affect the treatment and experiences of students non-Latino.

One of the particular experiences common to Latinos is discussed by legal scholar Kevin Johnson (Johnson, 1997; Johnson, 2000): being seen by the dominant society as being "different" and as bringing something "foreign to the Anglo-Saxon core." (1997, p.117) Johnson argues that this "foreignness" is seen not only as an assault on the normative American identity but also as defiance by Latinos who fail to assimilate to American's Anglo-Saxon core. Ultimately, Johnson argues, this failure to assimilate causes American society to blame *all* Latinos for all larger social problems in American society. This type of blaming, LatCrit theorists argue, has created inequitable legal and educational situations for all members of the Latino community, including long-time U.S. citizens and foreign-born immigrants. Johnson asserts that the lumping together of all Latinos as foreigners reveals the anti-Latino attitude of American society. Ultimately, LatCrit wants to eradicate the negative stereotypes that have been created about both foreign-born and

American-born Latinos in U.S. society, and to create more equitable opportunities for the entire Latino community.

LatCrit and CRT scholars share a pan-ethnic and pan-racial identity approach, but they also recognize the importance of moving away from fixed and controlled identities, which disregard the "multiplicity of identities held by members of any group." (Carter, 2005, p.162) While this research defined the undocumented immigrant student as "Mexican, undocumented and first-generation college student," my analysis is specific to Sunder Crossings, North Carolina and to the students who participated in the research. Even within this small sample, the uniqueness of these five individuals displays the dangers of lumping people and communities together. This book attempts to stress their common struggles without blurring their own individual life experiences and identities.

Choosing to use CRT and LatCrit in tandem is a powerful method that multiple scholars have used in the past (Delgado-Bernal, 2002; Delgado-Bernal & Solórzano, 2001; Fernandez, 2002; Valdes, 1998; Yosso, 2006). Using both CRT and LatCrit allows my theoretical framework to highlights the issues of race and racialization as central to lived experiences of people of color. Analyzing the experiences of undocumented Mexican immigrants shines a spotlight on people who have historically shunted to the lowest level of the hierarchy of American society. CRT and LatCrit together allow me both to research undocumented students and also to privilege their voices inside the research discourse.

CONCEPTUAL FRAMEWORK

While CRT provides a theoretical framework for this book, there are several key concepts that will give structure to the research. These organizing concepts provide powerful language with which to connect my framework to my analysis, and they enrich the findings. The questions posed regarding undocumented immigrant student identity, the role that school and teachers play in the college search process, and the questions of general access to higher education will be magnified through these various lenses.

Label of Other

In "How does it feel to be a problem? Education in the New Latino South," Murillo (2002) paints a complex picture of how the influx of

Latino newcomers to Sunder Crossings, NC[9] constructed a public sphere that labeled recent Latino immigrants as "problems," and therefore less deserving. Murillo interprets this "label of other" as a way to discipline immigrants in Sunder Crossings. Murillo builds his case through the evidence of poor treatment of Latino newcomers by the government, the education system and the general public. He emphasizes that the power structures in Sunder Crossings descend not only from the historic colonialism of the United States, but also from the particularly oppressive nature of the South. Murillo emphasizes that people in the town do not want their resources threatened or jeopardized by this new population of people which they see as "illegal" and "undeserving" of those public resources.

In her research on undocumented immigrants in New York City, Jocelyn Solis (2004) used a Vygotskian psychological perspective to explore the label of "illegal," arguing that human beings function and develop in a dialectical social relationship with the world around them:

> On entering the United States immigrants are identified and must identify themselves according to the legal terms that are available to them …consequently despite their irregular status they are unaware that they do have rights and they fail to stand up for them as a result of their illegal status and fear of deportation." (Solis, 2002, p.183).

She argues that undocumented immigrants understand their own reasons for being "illegal" and that, through the help of advocacy organizations, such as the *Asociacion Tepeyac*, where she conducted her research, they can defend their own illegal status and advocate for themselves. Relying on human rights and social justice the undocumented immigrants in Solis's research argued for their "legality" in terms of the daily economic and cultural contributions they made to U.S. society.

Althusser's (1971) concept of interpellation will be of significant use to understanding whether the label or being named "illegal" is a barrier for these students. The concept of interpellation can be explained by articulating that ideologies call or label people as subjects. Interpellation posits that in the moment that you are hailed or named and you turn around and respond, you have become a subject who is both a free

---

[9] The research conducted by Murillo occurred in the same town I conducted my research, thus I used Murillo's pseudonym so our research could be linked.

individual and a person who is subject to the law. The power of interpellation is that a person believes that they at some level have chosen to respond, yet in the moment of recognition, "you are an illegal", as someone accepts the label or title offered to them, they submit to the State.

As Althusser (1971) suggests, the power of naming someone transforms individuals into subjects. This research examines if the labels applied to undocumented students render them inferior to their American counterparts. The research explores whether the naming of undocumented student as "lawbreakers," "illegal aliens" or other derogatory labels constitutes them as subjects (lawbreakers) in their community. I also question whether they accept these derogatory labels and the effects such acceptance has on both K-12 and higher education.

Additionally, Murillo's negative "label of other" is juxtaposed with Suárez-Orozco's (1989) "dual frame of reference," which is said to positively affect academic achievement for immigrant students. This dual frame makes immigrant students evaluate what their life would be like back in their country of origin and rationalize that their life in the United States is much better; therefore, they are motivated to do well in school and to attempt to assimilate into American lifestyle. At the same time, other researchers have emphasized that many immigrant students are disappointed to find out that learning English or doing well in school does not constitute acceptance into American society (Olsen, 1997). This book examines where my students position themselves between their academic and cultural identities and how their status as undocumented affects these two differing identities. Do they see multiple identities as competing interests or as overlapping identities? Does their identity influence whether or not they apply to college?

Forms of Power
I also explore how different concepts of power help define the types of relations and relationships that are exercised within the school, community and college environment. While power is viewed by some as relational and diffuse (Focault, 1980; Focault, 1991), others see power as a hegemonic form of domination that keeps society socially and economically stratified (Bowles & Gintis, 1976). As I examine power in the school, I want to understand the general 'regimes of truth' regarding who does and who does not have access to higher education, and how these regimes are imposed throughout the college exploration process, and specifically with how the federal or state-level DREAM Act bills

could change the 'productions of truth' to help give undocumented students access to in-state tuition.

As this research takes a critical lens towards the difficulty of navigating the higher education system as an undocumented student, I would be remiss if I did not mention the influence of Paulo Freire's (1970) work on our understanding of power and agency. For Freire (1970), in order for the oppressed to "wage the struggle for their liberation, they must perceive reality of oppression not as a closed world from which there is no exit, but as a limiting situation which they can transform." (p.49)   Freire believed that everyone had the chance to transform their own world and through the process of *conscientazation* this would occur.   Once *conscientazation* occurred, people had the capacity to practice agency in the world and to control their own realities. For Freire everyone had the ability to possess the power to transform their own world and to ultimately make the world a better place. While Freire posits that personal agency is possible, and while this research recognizes that hope remains, the current structures and anti-immigrant fervor in the United States make it nearly impossible to make changes by and for these undocumented students.

Resisting Against Power
The students' stories also reveal how students and the teachers they worked with employed innovative practices of resistance against the system in different and varying manners.   This final piece of the conceptual framework looks at how authors have conceptualized both domination and resistance to power.

In *Domination and the Arts of Resistance,* James Scott (1990) argues that the relationship of discourse to power is most evident in the differences between the public and hidden transcript.   For Scott, the "public transcript" is the public performance required of people through many systematic forms of social subordination, and the "hidden transcript" takes place offstage beyond the direct observation of those in power.   Scott argues that, in public, people mask their true feelings and that subordinate groups find subtle ways to transmit their message.   The hidden transcripts of people not only are speech acts but a whole range of practices that are used against those in power.

Scott's work highlights the importance of public performances of loyalty and deference, and the power-laden situations of willing, which he argues are even "enthusiastic consent," by the subordinate.   This public behavior is evident in the treatment of teachers and school personnel, but this research also investigates whether undocumented students practice hidden transcripts when out of the spotlight of school and if they consider applying to colleges to be an act of defiance.

The work of Michel de Certau (1984) is particularly helpful in understanding and describing some of the actions that undocumented students employ in navigating the college application process. For de Certau, those in power use "strategies" to wield their power and influence others. The current laws in North Carolina which prohibit students without citizenship to gain access to in-state tuition might be considered one strategy for maintaining their second-class citizenship and keeping cheap labor force available in North Carolina. On the other hand, those who are subordinate, or "weak," utilize tactics to try and gain power. de Certau demonstrates how those with less power manipulate the system to their advantage. Rather than subverting the order and the structure of the system, they use the constraining order in creative ways to take advantage in the moments of "cracks" in the system when those in power have a momentarily lapse of control. These tactics, which de Certau calls the "space of the other" can be exemplified by ways that undocumented students have navigated the college application process, in some cases been admitted to university, and at the same time carefully controlled the number of people in their school community who know about their documentation status.

In *Examining Transformational Resistance Through a Critical Race and LatCrit Theory Framework: Chicana and Chicano students in an Urban Context* Solórzano and Delgado-Bernal (2001) identify four different types of oppositional behavior practiced by Chicano students.

1) Reactionary resistance: Students lack both a critique of their oppressive conditions and the motivation for social justice.
2) Self-defeating resistance: Students acknowledge their social conditions but ultimately engage in self-defeating behaviors.
3) Conformist resistance: Students are motivated by a need for social justice yet hold no critique of the system of oppression.
4) Transformational resistance: Students hold both a critique of oppression and a desire for social justice, and they are motivated to do something about their own personal situation. (316).

In addition Tara Yosso added a fifth behavior of "resilient resistance" where students are motivated by their own critiques, they act in the world on those critiques, and are "surviving and succeeding through the educational pipeline as a strategic response to visual micro aggressions." (Yosso in Solórzano & Delgado-Bernal, 2001, p.320)

Solórzano and Delgado-Bernal (2001) further explain that, in addition to these five "levels of resistance," their exist two different "categories of resistance": 1) Internal resistance with which students appear to conform to the norms of their community and school, yet are engaged in a critique of this society through more subtle and covert mannerisms. "On the surface his/her behavior appears to conform to societal and maybe parental expectations (p.325)," yet they are practicing strategies of resistance behind closed doors. 2) External resistance in which students do not necessarily conform to institutional norms and more visibly operate outside the traditional systems and accepted behaviors expected of them. Unlike Scott's concept of hidden transcripts, these students perform overt behaviors (vocal opposition, political writing, etc) to bring attention to their critique of the system.

CHAPTER 4

The Use of Critical and Reflexive Ethnography

This book highlights a year-long qualitative study focusing on five undocumented Mexican-immigrant high school students, and six teacher allies who had worked with these students during their time in high school and through the college exploration process. Additional data was collected on the policies and laws concerning undocumented immigrants in the state of North Carolina, on the public reception to them (in the form of newspaper articles, on-line forums and general responses to HB 1183), and on North Carolina university and community college responses to undocumented students.

The design of my study followed critical (Valenzuela and Foley, 2002) and reflexive ethnography (Davis, 1999), and narrative inquiry as conceptualized by Clandenin & Connelly (Clandenin & Connelly, 2000; Clandenin & Connelly, 2003).

CRITICAL AND REFLEXIVE ETHNOGRAPHY

While using CRT and LatCrit theoretical frameworks it was also extremely important to try to portray the lives of the students with accuracy and sensitivity, so both critical and reflexive ethnographic practices were employed in the research. Critical ethnography (Valenzuela & Foley, 2002) and post-critical ethnography (Noblit, Murillo, & Flores, 2004) both attend to avoiding the colonizing nature of ethnography by paying particular attention to the line between the powerful and the powerless. Critical ethnography replaces the grand narratives (Bhatkin, 1986) and recognizes that researchers always speak from a historically, politically, and culturally situated standpoint. Since there are multiple ways of knowing, individual ethnographies are only partial truths (Haraway, 1988) told from the viewpoint of the researcher who has written the ethnography.

Within critical ethnography, researchers such as Angela Valenzuela practice a type of research defined as participatory action research (PAR), which involves collaborating with participants and acting as a "cultural broker" between them and institutional structures. Since I helped the undocumented students as they tried to navigate the college process, ran a college prep program to help all Latino students at their high school, and worked with advocacy groups in the area to help increase support for passage of an in-state tuition legislative measure, my research was in-line with PAR. Taking a standpoint that nothing about research or education is politically neutral, an ethnographic practice that reflects this position was necessary.

Reflexive ethnography was also an important tool because it recognizes that that there is "always a place from which we speak."(Betty, 2003, p.23). Reflexive ethnography (Davies, 1999) forced me to reflect upon my place in the world and my relationship with the students, both before and after they found out whether or not they were going to be able to attend college, and in the follow-up after their senior year concluded. Reflexive ethnography (Davis, 1999) takes into considerations the multiple worlds that are inhabited by the researcher and the lives of the participants. It makes the researcher focus on the ethical concerns of conducting research and of constantly renegotiating the relationships that we have with our participants. Reflexive ethnography also avoids speaking from the ethnographic present and recognizes my research as situated within a context, part of a historical moment. I was especially mindful of this since I was in a community where past scholars had worked (Murillo, 2002; Vasquez, Seales & Marquardt, 2006; Villenas, 1996). While previous scholarship provided a powerful reflection on Sunder Crossings' past, I also considered that the research I conducted occurred during a different moment and place in time in the history of this community.

Reflexive ethnography can become a downward spiral into complete self-absorption. In the end some might argue that all we can learn from our research is something about ourselves, yet for me this was not enough. As a scholar who believes that there is importance in academic scholarship, in policymaking, and in the role of the practitioner, spiraling into complete self-absorption would be a disgrace to the commitment I have made to this community of students. While acknowledging my personal positionality, and agreeing with the postcolonial critique of self-absorption, reflexive ethnography (Davis, 1999) allowed me to find a balance in my research.

NARRATIVE INQUIRY

Methods of narrative inquiry (Clandenin & Connelly, 2000; Clandenin & Connelly, 2003) help illuminate the lived stories of the students and teacher allies. In narrative inquiry stories are viewed as cultural artifacts that are shaped by the context in which the story is shared. To utilize narrative inquiry, the researcher must pay particular attention to 1) the continuity of time (past, present and future) for the participants in the setting, 2) the interaction between the personal and the social, and 3) the context of place.

Utilizing narrative inquiry creates space to practice reflexive ethnography techniques which stress that we are all implicit in the world we research. Narrative inquiry stresses that there is no set rule for how something should look or be. The work transformed and reconfigured itself into numerous difference landscapes throughout the study. Because the lives of the students and the policies surrounding the status of undocumented students can change quickly, this element of narrative inquiry was particularly useful.

Narrative inquiry also stresses the dynamic of unequal power relations between the researcher and the participants. My role was as a privileged researcher who came into these students' lives at my convenience. I had to be always mindful of the reciprocity I provided not only for my students, but also for the greater high school community in Sunder Crossings.

One of the strengths of narrative inquiry is that there is no grand narrative or complete truth found from this type of inquiry research; rather, it is the lived experience and ethnography of the particular (Abu-Lughod, 1991), which I strived to create. Narrative inquiry has been criticized for being an ambiguous approach to research, to which it responds by demanding rigor in the data collection and methodology to combat what some view as the subjective nature of the work. There are *better* interpretations that exist in narrative inquiry because of attention to field methods and connecting theory to data analysis. These *better* interpretations include recognizing that who I am affects what I observe, that I must be prepared and focused when attending to the research setting. I must continually pay mindful attention to the data collected, the analysis of that data, and the theories utilized.

RESEARCH SITES AND PARTICIPANTS

The town of Sunder Crossings is located approximately 45 miles from a major city in North Carolina. It is a rural, working-class community. Many people in the community are employed at a national-brand poultry plant, and the Latino immigrant population in the community moved to this area in large numbers nearly 15 years ago in response to work opportunities at that poultry plant. Many Latino immigrants in Sunder Crossings are now employed at both the poultry plant and in construction. The growth of Latino students in the public schools has been dramatic. While 15 years ago, less than five percent of the high school were Latino students, in 2006 BGHS now comprised nearly 31 percent Latinos, 27 percent African-Americans, and 42 percent whites. Although the school was not allowed to inquire into students' documentation status, ESL teachers, counselors, and other school personnel estimated that a significant portion of the Latino student population at the high school was undocumented.

As director of a small academic mentoring program, the Latino Outreach Club (a pseudonym), for Latino students at BGHS, I met the group of seniors in the high school who would become the focus of this research in their junior year. I used "purposeful convenience sampling" by having teachers in the school help identify five first-generation, Mexican-origin, college-ready (defined as taking at least two honors courses since their sophomore year of high school), undocumented immigrant high school seniors. While individual participants represented a unique set of background experiences, including their journeys across the US/Mexico border and their early schooling experiences, they shared a common interest in continuing their education beyond high school.

All five participants were Mexican-origin undocumented immigrants. The sample consisted of three boys and two girls all of whom were 18 years of age, and one 17-year-old, whose guardians permitted her participation. Participant #1 (Saul) was a male born in

Veracruz, who had come to the United States at the age of 11. Participant #2 (Frances) was a female who was born in Guerrero and had traveled back and forth several times to the United States and finally settled in Sunder Crossings at the age of 15. Participant #3 (Carmen) was a female from Veracruz who had also moved to the United States at the age of 11. Participant #4 (Ricardo) was a male who had moved to the United States from Jalapa at seven years of age. Participant #5 (Fidel) was a male originally from the state of Veracruz who had moved to the United States at the age of 11. All of the participants had taken ESL coursework at some point during their public schooling, and all were now in only mainstream and honors classes.

In the interviews, students were asked to identify adults in their lives who had encouraged them or assisted them in learning about higher education, as well as people in their North Carolina community who had tried to help them or had encouraged them to consider going to college. This "snowball sampling method" produced a list of six BGHS teachers who were invited to participate in the study. Ally #1 (John) was a teacher who had been working at the school for four years. Ally #2 (Olivia) was a teacher who had been working at the school for over 20 years. Ally #3 (Jennifer) had been teaching at the school for three years. Ally #4 (David) had been working at the school for five years. Ally #5 (Carlos) had taught at BGHS for the last five years. Ally #6 (Stacey) had taught at the school for three years. These teachers served multiple roles at the school, including college counseling, acting as faculty advisors for student groups, and coaching sports teams at the school.

In building my relationships with these students and teachers, I emphasized my role as a graduate student at a research university in the state, and as a director of the mentoring program which had operated in their school for three years. Because gaining access to them while classes were in session was forbidden, I spent much of my time in places and during activities that occurred after school including: activities with the mentoring program I directed, an after-school leadership club, and extra-curricular activities. I also observed at community events like an immigration rally and soccer games, and I made weekly trips to Sunder Crossings where I spent time with the students in the public library, stores, restaurants, and their homes.

Two in-depth interviews were conducted with the students in the spring of their senior year. Semi-structured interview questions encouraged the students to discuss their schooling experiences in both Mexico and the United States, their interest and understanding of applying to college, and their lived experiences as undocumented immigrants living in the United States.[10]

Interviews were also conducted with the teacher allies. During these interviews, semi-structured questions encouraged them to discuss working with undocumented high school students (how they became aware that a student was undocumented, what they tried to do to help students who were undocumented, what they believed should be done regarding undocumented immigrant students and access to higher education).[11]

In the school district, which encompasses a county with more than 57,000 people and 15 schools in 2007, BGHS has long been the high school with the largest number of Latino high school students. The school receives Title I funding for its low-income student population, and the ESL population ranged between 75-100 students each year. Five full-time staff ran the ESL program on an inclusion model. A "newcomer program" kept new immigrant students in sheltered classes for approximately six months to a year, and then immigrant students were placed in all "regular" classes, with the exception of one ESL course. The school had nine AP courses, and students selected the career track (vocational, college prep, etc.) they wanted to follow; honors and AP courses were available to any student who chose to take them. The school was the first high school in the county to receive Latino immigrant students and still had the largest immigrant student population in the county in 2007. The teachers and administrators took pride in their school's proactive response to the new student population, something they claimed other schools in the county had difficulty doing.

DATA COLLECTION

Data collection for this project began officially in November 2005 and concluded in December 2006. Using ethnographic methods of data collection and analysis, I took detailed field notes of all observations and tape-recorded a reflective field log, all of which I wrote up in weekly field notes (Davies, 1999; Emerson, Fritz, & Shaw, 1995;

---

[10] See Appendix B for student interview protocol.

[11] See Appendix B for teacher interview protocol.

Glesne, 1999). Data collection entailed individual interviews with student and teacher allies, primary and secondary document review (including student transcripts, university policy manuals, and newspaper articles), and direct observation of Latino Outreach related events. The bulk of the individual interviews took place in spring 2006 of the participants' senior year; informal follow-up interviews, when possible, were collected in the fall. Further observations of school and Latino Outreach events occurred in the months of September, October, and November 2006. The trustworthiness of this inquiry was established through my prolonged engagement in the field, my persistent observation in multiple contexts, and my constant reflection as a researcher.

Writing Ethnographic Fieldnotes (Emerson & Shaw, 1995) influenced the continual process of moving in and out of the field for fieldnote collection. Taking fieldnotes and conducting interviews are processes wherein researchers constantly develop new insights and understandings. The researcher must sometimes move to the outside or to the margins in order to develop such understandings. Ultimately, ethnographic write-ups are subjectively selected by ethnographers as the most important. As the ethnographer, I decided what stories had priority and which did not. During the write-up of the research, I constantly reminded myself of how much influence I had on and how much I had co-constructed the stories told through my research.

To provide counter-narratives of the undocumented student experience, my first set of interviews focused on their journey to the United States and their educational trajectory both in Mexico and in North Carolina. In order to contextualize their counter-narratives, I collected data during a three-week research trip to Mexico, in the summer of 2006, to understand the lives students left behind and the types of experiences that would await them should they return to Mexico following high school graduation.

Information about the teacher allies who attempted to help these students were gathered through individual interviews and observations of the allies working with the student participants.

This ethnographic case study of students at Benson Guthrie High School also explores how official policies toward the undocumented Mexican population in the United States affected the lived experiences of these students. Since prior to this work, no research had been conducted on undocumented students living in a state that does not give these students access to in-state tuition, this research contextualized the problem better by answering some of the basic questions about what policies existed in North Carolina regarding access to higher education at individual colleges and institutions. In an attempt to highlight the limited policies, laws, and statistics available on undocumented immigrants, I referred to reports provided by North Carolina Latino advocacy groups, the Mexican Consulate in Raleigh, state data reports on education statistics, and media coverage regarding the attempted passage of HB 1183.[12] Since there was no statewide policy allowing undocumented students to attend universities (with the exception of the UNC system), I also contacted individual institutions to ascertain their policies on undocumented student applicants.

DATA ANALYSIS

Emerson & Shaw (1995) attest that interpreting and presenting participants' stories is the most difficult part of the research process. *Narrative Analysis* (Reissman, 1993) shows how one collects fieldnotes, observations, interviews and artifacts, and begins the process of analytic induction. Reismann stresses that persuasiveness in analysis requires linking theoretical claims not only to the data collected, but to the methodologies used to collect that data.

Once the final data collection was complete, qualitative software (*ATLAS.ti*) was used to analyze the content for themes and patterns and examine them in relation to existing data and literature about the undocumented student experience. The general thematic analysis for the students looked at their different experiences trying to access the college trajectory, while trying to understand what role being undocumented played in those experiences. The general thematic analysis for the teachers involved looking at how each of them had worked with and advised undocumented students, and their feelings regarding the school communities' reception of undocumented students.

Afterwards, themes and patterns were analyzed in relation to existing data and literature about the transnational and undocumented student experience. Grounding on the general thematic analysis, the data was next approached from my theoretical premises (CRT and

---

[12] HB 1183 was North Carolina's state version of the DREAM Act which would have allowed undocumented high school students to attend public universities for in-state tuition. For more details see Chapter 5 on policies in North Carolina.

LatCrit) to understand whether undocumented Mexican students' race and citizenship status create obstacles in the college application process.

While informal analysis was an ongoing part of this qualitative inquiry, a more formal and concentrated period of thematic analysis began in the fall after the data collection phase ended. During this more formal analysis, I organized relevant categories and themes which arose out of the field texts, interviews, and secondary data collected and I took into account not only the former research already conducted in Sunder Crossings (Murillo, 2002; Vasquez, Seales & Marquardt, 2006; Villenas, 1996), but also the ways in which the research site has changed over time in order to give a context to the histories of the participants I researched.

My analysis was finally subjected to a micro lens focusing on the lived experience of the students, and to a macro level analysis of the law and policy regulations that prohibit undocumented students from accessing higher education. In order to do this analysis it was necessary to address not only each individual student, the school community, and the town of Sunder Crossings, but also the political and social climate in the state of North Carolina towards undocumented immigrants.

After working on drafts of the analysis chapters I wanted to let my participants read the chapters, particularly those on resistance and identity formation, and to give critical feedback on whether my observations and interpretations were accurate. Fidel was interested in reading the chapters and expressed enthusiasm about providing honest and critical (if necessary) feedback. By conducting this member check (Stake, 1995) I was able to enrich the interpretations, and was provided encouragement that I was providing an accurate picture of "their" truth. During the final analysis stage I also spent a significant amount of time scrutinizing the drafts of my analysis chapters. During this time I focused also on analyzing interviews, field notes, and secondary data and this is where analytic induction will really come into play. As Bettie (2003) claims, "Persuasiveness (of research) is greatest when theoretical claims are supported with evidence from informant accounts and when alternative interpretations of the data are considered." (p.23) The process of connecting my theoretical and conceptual framework with the data was of particular importance as I moved forward in my final product. I hope that the book reveals that I not only utilized theory, but that I was also able to use CRT and LatCrit and my key theoretical concepts to advance the conversation on undocumented students.

LIMITATIONS

The biggest limitation of this research was that because of the vulnerability of the population selected, identifying a large sample population was difficult. The time and trust required to identify even five undocumented participants took a full 12-months. The invisibility of the population, and the fact that neither the school systems nor the United States government can collect data on them, would make it extremely difficult to use this research to create policy reform. The illegality of collecting data on undocumented students in the school is something that protects undocumented students as much as it keeps them subordinate. We simply don't know exact numbers of undocumented students in North Carolina. This limited the research's demographic profile for the purpose of contextualization.

Choosing to identify college-ready undocumented students narrowed an already small pool even further. This book explores the experiences of students that had strong academic identities, and were encouraged throughout their schooling experiences in the United States, it is my hope that future research will explore the undocumented student population who is not positioned in school in such a favorable manner. Students who are more recent immigrants, speak English with more difficulty, and are not identified as academically capable, experience the school system in a dramatically different way. This book does not capture that experience.

Finally, combining "ethnography of the particular" with an examination of law and policy, I also limit the generalizabilty of the data. The hope was that by creating chapters that illuminate the structural determinism of the laws and policies in the state of North Carolina, along with the power of the voice of the students' experiences, this book has the possibility to honor student lives, and to create research that displays the real individuals who are deeply affected by the current laws regarding undocumented immigrants.

CHAPTER 5

Broken Promises, Wasted Promise: How North Carolina's College Admission and Immigration Policies Prove Hollow

> Where there is a substantial economic disparity between two adjoining countries and the potential destination country promotes de jure or de facto access to its substantially superior minimum wage, that promotion encourages migrants reasonably to rely on the continuing possibility of migration, employment, and residence, until a competitive economic alternative is made available in the source country. (I. Lopez, 1981, p.1105)

As I walked down the cobblestone streets past the *tortilleria* in Pahuatlan, a small town high in the Sierra del Norte of Puebla, Mexico I hear the loud grinding of the two tortilla-making machines that sit behind the counter. The young student, who looks not much older than those I have been working with in Sunder Crossings, stands at the end of the machine staring into the distance. Her job is to stack the warm, fresh corn tortillas in bundles of nearly 100 or more, wrap them up in paper casing, and place them on the table behind her. Occasionally a chunk of dough stops the process, and she pauses to fix the machine. A young man nearly her age arrives to collect her stacks and deliver them to the local towns nearby. She continues stacking and wrapping, stacking and wrapping, as the drone of the loud machines fills the streets.

Intrigued by this young girl, I stop and ask if I can speak with the owner of the *tortilleria*. A friendly man comes out and introduces himself. I ask him to tell me about his business, and he states with pride the successes of his *tortilleria*, one of the more stable, money-making ventures in the community. When I inquire about the workers in his shop, he explains that he pays very fair wages (approximately $70.00 dollars per week). He only hires students who have graduated from *preparatoria* (the equivalent of high school in the United States). Students who have more education than their counterparts are best suited to work with the machines should they, as I had seen earlier, have any problems or get jammed up. The owner explains that working at his *tortilleria* is one of the few secure, well-paying jobs in the community. I turn back to see the young woman continuing her task of stacking and wrapping, stacking and wrapping. I thank the man for taking the time to visit with me, and with a generosity that has come to be the norm on my visit to Puebla, he hands me a stack of tortillas fresh off the conveyor belt. I walk away from the store front, and can't help but think of the students I work with at Benson Guthrie High School who might be here had their families not left for work in *Carolina del Norte*.

OFFICIAL POLICIES IN NORTH CAROLINA[13]

North Carolina is a state that does not provide in-state tuition for undocumented students. In spring 2005, House Bill 1183, "Access to Higher Education and a Better Economic Future" was introduced and would have allowed undocumented immigrants who had graduated from a North Carolina high school and met the residency requirements

---

[13] For an estimate of undocumented high school students in North Carolina please see Appendix C

of the state to pay in-state tuition. Due to the vocal outcry of anti-immigrant groups, the bill never left the Education Committee of the North Carolina House of Representatives. No bill on in-state tuition has been introduced into the House or Senate since this legislation was killed in committee in 2005.

Beyond the state-sponsored prohibition of in-state tuition policies for undocumented students, the policies for admitting undocumented immigrant students vary among public and private universities, and community colleges in North Carolina. In 2004 the University of North Carolina system (including 16 campuses across the state), adopted an official policy to allow undocumented students to apply to the statewide system, but to disallow any further aid. This policy reads:

> 700.1.4: Undocumented aliens are eligible to be considered for admission as undergraduates at institutions based on their individual qualifications with limitations as set out below:
>
> 1. An undocumented alien may be considered for admission only if he or she graduated from high school in the United States.
> 2. Undocumented aliens may not receive state or federal financial aid in the form of a grant or a loan.
> 3. An undocumented alien may not be considered a North Carolina resident for tuition purposes; all undocumented aliens must be charged out of state tuition.
> 4. All undocumented aliens, whether or not they abide in North Carolina or graduate from a North Carolina high school, will be considered out of State for purposes of calculating the 18% cap on out of State freshmen pursuant of Policy 700.1.3.
> 5. When considering whether or not to admit an undocumented alien into a specific program of study, constituent institutions should take into account that federal law prohibits the states from granting professional licenses to undocumented aliens. (University of North Carolina Policy Manual, 2006)

While the UNC system holds an official policy for its 16 member campuses, and North Carolina State University upholds a similar policy, but did not have it published in written form, private universities and community colleges can set their own policy regarding admission of undocumented students. The North Carolina Community College System, however, officially declared that, "Local community colleges have the discretion to implement admission policies that permit the enrollment of undocumented immigrant applicants to curriculum, continuing education and basic skills programs. Undocumented immigrants do not qualify for in-state tuition and shall be charged at the out-of-state tuition rate for curriculum programs" (NCSHP, 2006). Private universities and community colleges in the state must be contacted individually for admission about eligibility for undocumented immigrant students.

These policies undercut the possibility of higher education for undocumented students. Students and their teacher allies work to overcome these obstacles but often face purposive structural determinisms.

As highlighted earlier, numerous scholars have written about the racialized and discriminatory nature of immigration law and policy (Olivas, 1995; Olivas, 2005; Motomura, 2006; Ngai, 2004). Along with immigration scholars, education historians have routinely described the obstacles faced by Latino students in the public education system (Donato, 1997; Gonzalez, 1990; San Miguel, 1987). Because the issue of undocumented students accessing higher education is framed by issues of race and ethnicity, a theory that highlights the centrality of race in American society is appropriate. Using critical race theory (CRT) and Latino Critical Theory (LatCrit) allows for interpretation and critique of the experiences of undocumented students who are denied access to higher education because of their Mexican-immigrant background.

Working from the standpoint that undocumented students do possess strengths and should be valued for their bicultural and bilingual capital, structural determinism (Delgado, 1995; Tate, 1997) helps explain how current legal barriers, by reason of their structural limitations, prevent undocumented students from moving beyond a 12th grade education. While the Plyer v. Doe decision grants access to the K-12 education system, the current legal system does not help transnational students from moving beyond this point. The law, and the resistance to passing legislation such as the DREAM Act, maintains the status quo. Researching the experiences of undocumented Mexican immigrants shines a spotlight on people who have historically been shunted to the lowest levels of the hierarchy of American society.

STUDENTS ARE COLLEGE-READY

The five students shared the personal characteristics of being Mexican-origin, college-ready high school seniors. These students came to the United States between the ages of 7-11, and had been educated in American public education system since the time they had arrived. Below is a chart that represents their academic backgrounds during their time in high school and later. The chart headings include the age they arrived in the United States, their class rank at the time of graduation, the number of honors courses they had taken since their freshmen year, the number of AP courses they had taken, their ACT score, and the academic track they were officially registered under on their transcripts. The final category shows what students were doing after they completed high school.

Figure 1: Students Academic Backgrounds

Name	Age of Arrival in U.S.	Class Rank	# of Honors (AP) Classes	ACT Score	H.S. Education Track	Post-H.S. Outcome
Fidel	11	18/136 (13%)	15(7)	26	College Prep	College/ 4-year
Ricardo	7	15/136 (11%)	14(2)	20	College Prep	Odd jobs
Carmen	11	46/136 (33%)	8(2)	21	Career Prep	Working fast food
Saul	11	39/136 (28%)	11(2)	17	College Prep	Working as welder
Frances	15/ varied	36/136 (26%)	7(0)	18	Career Prep	Returned to Mexico

This figure helps illustrate that each of these students had completed the necessary coursework to qualify for graduation from high school (including taking at least two honors courses each year), and for post-secondary opportunities. Each of the students had access to education because Plyer v. Doe mandates that states cannot deny free public education through grade 12 to undocumented children (Olivas, 2004;

Olivas, 2005). And each of the students would be able to apply to the UNC system, as well as other limited private and public colleges in the state that have policies allowing undocumented students to apply to their institution.

TEACHERS AS INSTITUTIONAL AGENTS

The existing structures impeded teachers from providing opportunities for their undocumented students, nevertheless, the teacher allies made valiant attempts to help the students and encourage them inside the school setting. In *Children of Immigration*, Suárez-Orozco and Suárez-Orozco (2001) comment that, "The "structures of opportunity" or, conversely, "fields of endangerment" that many children face are fundamental for understanding the paths that they choose in the new setting" (p.117).

Since none of the undocumented students had parents who had the cultural capital knowledge (Bourdieu, 1986) necessary for navigating the college application process in the United States, the teacher allies acted as institutional agents to these students (Stanton-Salazar, 1995; Stanton-Salazar, 1997; Stanton-Salazar & Spina, 2000; Stanton-Salazar & Spina, 2003). Stanton-Salazar (1997) defines institutional agents as "those individuals who have the capacity and commitment to directly transmit, or negotiate the transmission of, institutional resources and opportunities" (p.6). While later chapters demonstrate how students' parents encouraged them to do well in school, the immigrant parents' own experiences in Mexico created different educational expectations than those that occurred in North Carolina.

Teachers and students commented that they were able to get assistance at school from teachers when their parents were unable to provide this help. Parents were often unable to provide this help because of their lack of high-level English reading and writing skills. Mr. John, who frequently visited the homes of his students, provided several examples of how he helped his students when their parents were unable to do so.

> Mario (a pseudonym) has gotten into Campbell. We worked on his application together and his essay together and we worked on his financial aid, all sorts of things that no one in his family could do.

So I can guide them along with that. I can help with the essay and how you should structure the essay, and this kid doesn't have anybody at home to do that, so that's a real block. These kids they have the grades, but applying is a whole other block.

Those kids (with recent immigrant parents) are just self-educated, so they go home, and they do all their own homework. I did that too because my mom and dad couldn't help me with my homework. Most of them don't have a computer and Internet connection in their home; some of them come over to my house. Last time Saul was over we talked about Great Gatsby and Brave New World, but could his parents do that with him? No! We talked about the Great Gatsby, and I hadn't read it in a while, but it is fun for me because I can re-read the book with him and think about themes, and help him and provide a little bit more of a context.

While Mexican immigrant parents did their best to provide a supportive environment for their children, the teachers had the capital to provide access to knowledge regarding the expectations of honors coursework and the college application process. Throughout their junior and senior years I observed as the teacher allies helped their students write college essays, helped them fill out college and financial aid applications, and even took students on visits to college campuses. During their interviews students talked about how teacher allies, when parents were unable to fulfill this role, encouraged them in the college process.

Janet: Did people in your family help you out with your college applications?

Frances: No, it was only the teachers at school that helped me out.

Saul: You know when I came here as a freshman, I was excited about going to college. And he [Mr. John] told me that I really had the ability, a lot of people told me that I have the ability... My family: we never have really talked about college. My dad doesn't really know anything about college. I mean, he knows that I wrote letters about applying to college, and he knows that I have received some stuff from college, and all he does is give it to me, but we've never sat down and had a conversation. He has never said to me are you going to go to college?

Fidel: Well, I think that I told Ms. Olivia that I was undocumented, because I hadn't told her before, and she told Ms. Jennifer and then Ms. Jennifer started talking to me. And I didn't know Mr. David either until he learned that I had written a book, and then he started talking to me about my book and about me.

As comments above show, teachers became involved in students' lives, helping them apply to college when their parents were unable to do so, and encouraging students in all of their academic pursuits. Throughout the year, I observed teachers encourage the student participants to take more rigorous coursework, provide social networks to give access to other teachers in the school, and spend countless hours with numerous other students in the school. While teachers had little control over the policies that were enforced inside the school, they created agency when they rejected playing a passive role in adhering to any deficit perspectives about undocumented Mexican immigrant students. Despite the structural determinisms, the teacher allies' efforts and care for these students were notable.

In addition to being institutional agents the teacher allies, particularly the white teachers, also commented that working with these undocumented students had opened their eyes to the lived experiences of immigration and to the resiliency of the Latino community in Sunder Crossings. In an email regarding the growing pains of the Latino Outreach program, David shared his thoughts regarding what he had learned and gained from working with Latino immigrants at BGHS:

I first started working directly with immigrants 13 years ago. It's only been in the past three years that I've quit trying to save them. I used to think that their lives would be better if I could get them into college, build them a house, hell anything… it's just been recently that I'm starting to realize that their lives will go on successfully without us. Even our high school drop outs somehow find their niche in the world. It may not be the future that I would choose for them but for the most part they're happy. I'm only saying this because it affords us some wiggle room, the mistakes we make are not going to ruin their lives. The Latino Outreach could leave BGHS today and those kids would make it somehow. Maybe not a four year college but somehow they'll pull through. In some ways they are victims of a system, but no more than a lot of people have been throughout history. Still, if we can help, we should.

Teacher allies approached their work with undocumented students through various perspectives but all shared the collective sentiment that they had gained as much through their relationships with these students as they had given of their time and energy. The teacher allies that worked with the students in collective partnership rather than a savior and victim role found their lives changed along with the lives they were trying to change.

THE MYTH OF EQUAL OPPORTUNITY

The myth about various admission policies in North Carolina claim high school gives every student in the state the opportunity to accrue benefits (including attending college) from public education. The dominant ideology of the American public education system is that school is a place where every child (including undocumented children) will have access to equal opportunities for learning. At BGHS this claim is illustrated in their mission statement: "To prepare each individual student with self-esteem, confidence and responsibility necessary to meet the demands of independent living in a constantly changing society". This idea was repeated often when I spoke with school administrators regarding the school's response to the influx of Latino students nearly ten years ago. One administrator, during a public presentation, commented, "At BGHS, we tried to make sense of the issue and make sure that everyone received education. We have made room for all the students." Yet, the teacher allies recognized that undocumented students did not have the same access to the benefits of education because the policies regarding higher education in North Carolina were not equitable.

To this point a teacher commented, "So we don't care what race they are (here in the school), or what their background is, but we want all of them to push themselves to do the honors and AP if they are capable. So, now my Hispanic students have done well, now they're ready and they want to go to college, and that's where the barrier is. And you know they are ready to go to college and ready to do the work".

The school's mission and the promise of equal access to education proffer a false sense of equitable conditions for these children. Olivia, a teacher, commented, "I think that students build faith in the school because the law asks us to do it, to teach children, and we teach who shows up on our doorstep and who lives in our district. And we're, mercifully, not asked to make those excruciating kinds of decisions, so we are able to teach everyone."

While K-12 education perpetuates the myth that everyone is on equal footing, the policies for access to higher education, and even larger policies regarding citizenship status, undermine students and teachers attempts to post-secondary opportunities.

OUR HANDS ARE TIED

All of the teacher allies felt very passionately about undocumented children being granted access to in-state tuition. Their passions are reflected in the statement by Ms. Stacey, who said:

> I tell people that, when they look at my school they need to consider that my students did not come here on their own accord. They were brought here by their parents. If you want to blame anybody, blame the conditions in Mexico, blame the government, blame their parents, but please don't take it out on my students. These are my students, and every student at Benson Guthrie I am responsible for. I've been told on more than one occasion that I can't be responsible for all of my students, but I really feel that the government has to take some responsibility on this issue.

Her feelings echoed those of other teachers, who wanted to help the students but felt that policies regarding undocumented immigrants and, more specifically the policies on undocumented immigrants and higher education completely controlled what they were able to do for the students they worked with each day. As a result, the teachers felt that current policies prohibited them from providing realistic or obtainable post-secondary options for their students.

Without any change or modification in immigration laws or higher education policies for immigrant students, these teachers were limited by the system they were attempting to operate within. Beyond these limitations, the teachers also felt constrained by policies regarding unauthorized immigration, including the obstacles that occurred from a student's not having a social security number, and the policies in North Carolina that allowed students to apply to university, but charged them out-of-state tuition.

The lack of a social security card (termed "a social" by school personnel) prohibited undocumented students from participating in several of the more successful pre-professional programs that operated at the high school. For example, BGHS had a very successful allied health program where students could complete an associate's degree in nursing by the time they graduated from high school; this option was unavailable to undocumented students. Several teachers commented on this situation, but one in particular gave voice to their frustration:

> One of the real wicked catches here is that one of the great programs we have here is the allied health, physical science medical program. There is absolutely no job you can get in the hospital without a valid social, and so you can't get into the community college program, and so you can't be a nurse, you can't be an LPN or a CNA, which is going to give a significantly better rate than minimum wage. You can actually graduate from this high school in the allied health program, and when you're finished you're a certified nursing assistant. So you could walk into a real job straight out of here if you have a real social.

Other professional programs at the school including a mechanics certificate and a cosmetology program had similar problems. Jennifer, a fierce advocate for the young women in the school, said, "You run into a lot of problems. Like, I know the Latina girls, a lot of them, do the cosmetology program, and they really seem to enjoy it, and it gives them work opportunities and independence after they leave school. They could easily set up shop for themselves or at home, but to pass the North Carolina cosmetology exam, to actually get your certificate, you have to write down a social security number."

Just as the students who might be preparing for technical or skilled trade jobs were prohibited from pursuing access to those opportunities, policies in the state regarding applying to college as an out-of-state student were unrealistic as well. Teachers who tried to help students navigate the system felt constrained by the financial barriers and the difficulty of the application process itself.

The policies that currently exist in the UNC system and at other various campuses in the state may allow students to apply, but with without access to financial aid the price-tag of a public four-year university is unrealistic. Many teachers expressed disappointment at the students' having to finance education without access to financial aid:

> Let me tell you what is the real killer is --the community college. A child's entire goal is to go to community college, to be a registered nurse, to get this good solid job, and they have to pay out of state tuition, and all the paperwork they have to complete.

> It makes me sad because being able to get in doesn't really help them at all, and I think the only way they might be able to do it is to pay out-of-state tuition and work full-time and maybe things might change in a couple years.

These thoughts were repeated about access to scholarship programs in the state and nation, the majority of which require that a student be a U.S. citizen. Ms. Stacey discussed the process of financial aid for undocumented students: "And the next thing I did with the student was talk to him about how he was going to afford to pay for college, and then I tried to give him a list of Hispanic scholarship websites. But I ran into the problem that most of those scholarships were only for Hispanic citizens."

The teachers at BGHS did not feel that piecemeal admission policies across the state represented an "access for all" model for their students. The organization of the policies and the difficulty of each individual policy made inquiring about or applying to college a difficult process, even for the undocumented students who were academically prepared to do so. As immigration scholar Michael Olivas (2004) commented, "...for these children, their lives in the shadows will likely meet the sharp light of the college application process, where substantial paperwork and documentation are prerequisites." (437)

The first difficulty for teachers who wanted to help these students involved figuring out which colleges would even consider accepting undocumented students. One teacher described her difficulty when contacting universities regarding a strong undocumented Latino male: "So I just start calling up a list of about 10 colleges, and one after another they just kept telling me there is nothing they could do because he is going to be out of state. They told me he was going to have to fill out the international student application." The next difficulty involved the process of applying as an international student, and being unable to provide the necessary information or paperwork for that designation as well. A teacher who worked directly with Fidel recalled the process for him: "So, he tried to begin the process of getting his Mexican passport, and trying to get his international application in order, which made the process, which was already full of a lot of obstacles, have even more to get through." Finally, applying as an international student also means that students must compete with the out-of-state student pool. At the University of North Carolina-Chapel Hill, the flagship institution of the state, this would mean competing with upwards of 11,000 students for only 2000 admission spots reserved for out-of-state students (From those admitted, the university expects to enroll around 650).

Although some universities will accept undocumented students, the current policy structure does not support a realistic model for access to higher education for the overwhelming majority of undocumented college-ready students. The current immigration policies leave students who want to work after high school crippled as well. Given the financial and logistical obstacles, teachers were left with few post-secondary or work options for their students. The few suggestions teachers made --taking jobs mowing lawns, babysitting, or working for businesses that were known to hire undocumented workers-- expose the myth of equal opportunity in the public education system, and relegate the undocumented students to the second class in U.S. society and, even worse, to the irregular economy that is characterized by low wages, no benefits, and uncertain continuation. While teachers believed that "there is a place in the North Carolina college system for all these kids," the state's policies do not support their opinion.

SOMETIMES IT FEELS WRONG

The teachers also recognized that the message sent to undocumented students by the schools --that they, too, could attend college like their American peers-- was simply untrue. Many, but not all, teachers understood the centrality of race in immigration laws, and all were frustrated by the situation. Mr. David a teacher and coach, remarked, "In high school I think there is a certain sense of a level playing field. But when I drive home my Latino kids to their trailer parks and I drive home my American middle-class students, you really see that their realities are totally different.... We want to show kids [through the Latino Outreach program] that university is not something reserved completely for white kids because that's the perception they see. Now in some ways it is ironic because we are lying to some of them because the opportunities for the undocumented Latino students are quite different than for those students who are citizens."

Teachers often felt trapped in the system and questioned encouraging students when the barriers were so difficult:

> Yes it makes me feel completely hopeless and it makes me feel sad when they see all of these motivational speakers and they are saying, "You can do it," and that's not really true.

> Sometimes it feels wrong because if you're saying just keep working at it, but in the back of your head, you know that maybe you're just lying to a kid. I mean there may be an opportunity, but really it may not be there.

> I think it's sort of a bittersweet prize, like here's your diploma and now sorry no more education.

While some felt hopeless, others got mad and argued the students' substantive membership rights (Perry, 2006) with other teachers and community members, and in lobbying their local government officials. Ms. Stacey remarked,

> I get mad and I email every congressman I can think of and I just get these form letters back. They might have someone call me and say that they are working on legislation on this issue, but they just pacify me, and it makes me mad because

> what I really want is for these children to be in college, because they are qualified.

Regarding the claim that these students are North Carolina residents Olivia commented,

> They pay property tax, you know seven percent of every dollar they earn goes to the state of North Carolina, and I think that the way residency requirements are written for universities, that these children qualify. Are they legal residents of the United States? No. Are they residents of North Carolina? Yes."

Despite the often valiant efforts the teachers made when working with undocumented students, the system currently prevents any innovative solution for college-ready undocumented students.

STRUCTURE OVER AGENCY

The discouragement felt by the teacher allies was summed up by Ms. Jennifer:

> I have a student with a great family, very supportive and I would guess they have come here with the attitude that this is the land of opportunity, so perhaps this is where her head is now. Here we are, and we can do it, and we can get ahead, perhaps, not realizing that in three years that if her family is undocumented those opportunities to study at college are going to drop tremendously.

This statement reveals not only the false promises of the North Carolina school system, but also the likelihood of a bitterly disillusioned future for the overwhelming majority of undocumented students currently living in North Carolina. Although current North Carolina college admission policies appear to create some level of access, they do not truly create full access for undocumented students at this given moment in history. These policies make college financially inaccessible, and create numerous obstacles throughout the application process. Without reconceptualizing policies to represent a more inclusive model for undocumented students, only a rare few may gain access to the higher education system. In addition, without policies that offer a path to citizenship, those rare students who have overcome the significant barriers to accessing higher education will not be able to use their degrees to find employment upon graduation from college.

The policies in North Carolina drastically affect the individual lives of undocumented students at Benson Guthrie High School. To provide more authentically equitable education experiences for undocumented students', researchers and policymakers must be willing to expose the claims of neutrality in the policies surrounding access to higher education for undocumented immigrants as falsehoods, and we must use that information to create innovative jurisprudence to reconceptualize the "illegality" of students stuck in a broken immigration system. The North Carolina economy asked for workers and with them came families who now call Sunder Crossings, and cities around the state their home. These children, as former Governor Jim Hunt suggested recently, are "North Carolina's children and God's children," and they are a gift, not a cross, for this state to bear.

CHAPTER 6

Academic, Transnational and Undocumented: Conflicting Identities in Motion

In *Narrating and Counternarrating Illegality as an Identity*, Jocelyn Solis (2004) argues, "Societal and personal discourses each tell a story that informs our thinking about undocumented immigrants, who they are in the United States, and what they do or do not deserve. These opposing, value-laden explanatory frameworks are defined as narratives of *conflict*." (183). Like Murillo (2002), Solis (Solis, 2002; Solis, 2004; Solis, 2005) contends that undocumented immigrants are given the label of "illegal" and are identified as less deserving of resources and human rights because of their documentation status. Murillo documented how the media's and communities' "othering" of the new Latino population positioned them as being less deserving in both their schools and local communities. While Murillo illuminated how the new community of Latino immigrants was given a position of subordination in Sunder Crossings, Solis showed how Mexican immigrants in New York City, with the help of an advocacy group, were able to create counternarratives to the label of "illegal" and to craft a new identity based on their economic and cultural contributions. While Murillo explored the notion of interpolation (Althusser, 1971) in a small, rural community that had no experience with Mexican immigrants, and Solis showed how undocumented immigrants countered the grand narratives (Bhatkin, 1984) created for them in the context of a large, urban city with a long history of immigration, this research articulates the discourses on undocumented immigrant identity that existed in 2006 in Sunder Crossings and Benson Guthrie High School.

Solis' (2004) use of the term "conflict"[14] seems an appropriate one for describing the multiple identities and multiple tensions that existed for each of the individual students in this book. Using LatCrit in addition to CRT also allows the exploration of problems and challenges unique to the Mexican undocumented community in Sunder Crossings, North Carolina. These problems include the grand narratives that are the residual effects of a town that did not desegregate its high schools until 1967, a town that still worships in ethnically segregated groups on Sundays, a town that had had little to no demographic change for nearly a hundred years, yet within a span of just a few years, received an entirely new community of people.

While it is important to contextualize the environment in Sunder Crossings with historical accounts and research from the past (Murillo, 2001; Murillo, 2002; Villenas, 2001), it also is important to emphasize that while this community is not like the immigrant receiving community of New York City, and likely never will be, Sunder Crossings has one of the better infrastructures in North Carolina for receiving new immigrants. In addition to an intake center which helps

---

[14]Narratives of conflict in Sunder Crossings include Murillo's depiction of a town that holds strong negative stereotypes about Mexican immigrants, up against teachers in this research study who believed that Mexican parents are more concerned for their children's well-being than white parents, and that Mexican immigrant students are the more intrinsically motivated as compared to their American counterparts.

new Latino immigrants register for school, makes them aware of any medical and other emergency services available to them and helps them find safe housing, there also is a Hispanic advocacy group that presses for immigrant rights and supports a community radio show, and a dual-language elementary school.[15] These offerings are present because the social network of Latino immigrants has grown enough so that friends and family have migrated to this community, and because jobs and other economic and social opportunities still exist for Latino immigrants here. While the "othering" that Murillo (2001) and Villenas (2001) described in past research clearly still exists, it is ten years later, and the community has changed. While some change has been positive and other change has been negative, the enduring struggles in this community live on (Holland and Lave, 2000). Even so, it is important to delineate precise ways in which the community is continually changing.

It is here, within a community that has undergone a significant amount of change in the past ten years, that the undocumented high school students considered and, in all cases but one, attempted to pursue higher education directly after high school. The words "conflict" or "conflicting" are appropriate for the multiple and varied identities of the undocumented students experienced as they attempted to pursue higher education. The identities enacted by the students, which could be considered part of their "history in person" (Holland & Lave, 2000), contain their own subjective life experiences. These identities arose from the experiences that the students had both at home and at school but also reflected the collective memories and experiences that their families and the Latino community have experienced in Sunder Crossings (Urrieta, 2003).

The self-identities of the students are constantly changing and, as multiple scholars have argued, are in a constant process of *becoming* (Holland & Lave, 2000, Urrieta, 2007). Identity is influenced by these students' varying positions, including their race, class, citizenship status, transcultural experiences and academic positions at school. Identity is affected by how the undocumented students are positioned in their school and later in the outside world, and also by how they decide

---

[15] The first dual-language class, starting with kindergarten-age children, began in the 2005-2006 school year.

to position themselves in relation to these two contexts. These identities contain both conceptual and procedural shifts, which according to both Holland et al. (1998) and Urrieta (2007) include the mental process of identity production (conceptual, i.e. telling themselves and others who they are) and the actions that make this identity real (procedural, i.e. acting in the world to embody this identity).

In his research with high-achieving American Indian students at Ivy League institutions, Bryan Brayboy (2004) challenged general theories of accommodation and assimilation by showing the complexity of how American Indian students at one private college, "position themselves in relation to others, and how the institution and its agents position them." (147) Brayboy showed how students simultaneously maintained their cultural and academic identities by making themselves either visible or invisible in different situations. Brayboy complicates the literature on accommodation and assimilation by showing that, while society creates labels and stereotypes for American Indians, the American Indian students in his research practiced purposeful agency by re-crafting the identities that had been created for them.

In his research on Chicana/o activist educators, Luis Urrieta (2003, 2009) explored how the context of different academic environments (from K-12, through undergraduate and graduate school) triggered the development of Chicano identity and consciousness. Urrieta described how the process of becoming Chicana/o was an individual process, varying from person to person, that was one of continual formation for his participants. Ultimately, he argued that Chicana/o identity formation for activist educators is encapsulated in their collective memory, their lived experiences, and their daily practices as activists in education systems.

Similar to both Brayboy (2004) and Urrieta (2003, 2009), I sought how kids position themselves and are positioned in relation to both their academic identity and their cultural (transnational) identity. In addition to these two identities, I wanted to understand how documentation status affected their multiple identities and positioned them. While the two identities of academic and cultural identity provide enough complexity by themselves, the additional identity of "undocumented" provides another layer for analysis. Among the students, there existed a wide and varied range in what they felt was possible to accomplish, what types of family backgrounds had been supporting them, why they chose to remain in school despite their immigration status, and with how much hope they envisioned their futures.

While multiple poles existed, the shuttling back and forth across the cultural boundaries became apparent in my thematic analysis. These poles included the home and school environment (including their Mexican and American identity), and the "undocumented" versus "illegal" dialectic. These conflicting identities were shaped by the majoritarian stories (Solórzano & Yosso, 2002) that were widely apparent in the media frenzy surrounding the immigration debate during the time of this research and were further emphasized in the community during a historic immigration rally/march in the spring of the students' senior year. Because of their age when they arrived in the United States, all of the students were aware of their undocumented status (and had a dual frame of reference), for they all had concrete memories of border-crossing. Yet, they each did not know that they would have difficulty attending college in the United States until they began exploring the idea of applying to college during their junior and senior years.

HOME VERSUS SCHOOL: DIFFERENT WORLDS

Before exploring how the identity of being undocumented intersects with academic and transnational cultural identity, it is important to first establish the distinct disconnection that exists between home and school for all of the students. While all of the students were encouraged to do well in school, their families did not feel welcome and had not established a presence in the school community, with the exception of attending soccer games. Some of the students cited language obstacles as one reason their parents did not feel welcome, others emphasized that parents' work schedules prevented them from being active during the school day or at after-school activities. Carmen mentioned that in Mexico her parents worked less and, thus, could spend more time together as a family, which facilitated their involvement in Mexican schooling. She commented, "Like, over there (in Mexico) families are very united, and your parents can spend more time with you, and here your parents have to work. They sometimes have two jobs; I mean you don't see them all the time." Carmen also felt that parents were not as welcome at the schools in the United States as they had been in Mexico, and because of this, they did not want to be involved at the high school.

Suárez-Orozco and Suárez-Orozco (2001) described the tightrope that many immigrant parents face when trying to encourage their children to do well in school, arguably the foundation of their new American culture, yet also to maintain the traditions and the language of home.   School is also the key socializing agent for immigrant students.

The students' parents attempted to temper the effects of what they perceived as negative American characteristics that were a result of their child's exposure to American culture at school.   While all the students maintained both their written and spoken Spanish language skills, their parents had had much more difficulty preserving the language and cultural traits in their younger (and sometimes American-born) siblings.   Several of the students mentioned the negative aspects their parents felt school caused in their younger siblings. An example of this from both the student's perspective and a teacher's perspective appears below:

According to Carmen:

> I have a little sister, and she's in a period of big change right now, different from what she was in Mexico. You can see in Mexico like a little sweet girl and now she's different. And then we moved to the city, and she changed a lot, she really started misbehaving in the new school she was in, her grades went down. She flunked. My parents say she's becoming more American.

Ms. Jennifer commented on what happened after immigrant students have been in the public school system for more than a year:

> And I think it's that they watch the others kids in the school and how they behave, not just the Latino kids, they watch all the kids, and they think that they can tell a teacher this or that in America and get away with it, or that I can get sent into a ISS (detention) for the day and I can sleep and not have to put up with my teacher, yes, that seems like a pretty good idea.

In addition to more general cultural differences between home and school, many of which have been supported by the work of other researchers (Valdes, 1996; Valdes, 1998; Valenzuela, 1999), most of the students experienced differing educational expectations at home versus at school. While all of the students' families encouraged them to do well in school, fewer of the parents encouraged their children to pursue education beyond a high school diploma. For both Carmen and Frances, a college education was encouraged as a chance to achieve at their highest potential. While Fidel was encouraged to do well in high school his family was aware that his documentation status would create a major obstacle to reaching that goal and did not want him setting himself up for failure; thus; encouraged him to think about a job after high school. In the cases of Ricardo and Saul, neither of their parents had encouraged them to attend college. Saul explained this as follows:

> I think the fact that I work and that I do the best that I can, and that I try to work and to go to school and to give my brother and sister things, I think that's what they expect of me. I help my dad out when he needs help. And that's why I think they believe that I'm a good son. Their expectations for me at school are that I graduate from high school, and I think that I believe that that was their highest expectation because they never really expected me to go to college.

For many of the students whose families came from remote, rural areas of Mexico, attending college had not been a possibility in their country of origin, especially since all came from low-income backgrounds. Many of the teachers emphasized this in their interviews, telling me that asking the kids about their college dreams in Mexico was an unrealistic question, given that their parents' educational experiences and expectations were vastly different than American parents'. As to that, Mr. John said,

> The question you asked the kids, it's an unfair question to ask about whether or not you thought about college in Mexico, because nobody does, you get up to the sixth grade, and that's it. It's a question of socioeconomic status, that's what your uncle and your cousins do, because you can't afford education after that point. You can't afford the school uniforms, education usually stops at that point, and everybody knows that.

Saul's family echoed Mr. John's reflections on Mexican parents' educational expectations:

> No, in my family we never have really talked about college;
> my dad doesn't really know anything about college. I mean,
> he knows that I wrote letters about applying to college, and he
> knows that I have received some stuff from college and all he
> does is give it to me, but we've never sat down and had a
> conversation. He never said to me are you going to go to
> college? It's not like an American family where they're
> pushing their son to apply to college or in a situation like well
> if you do well, on your grades or if you don't do well, I'll take
> away your car. That's not the way it operates in a Mexican
> family.

Some of the teachers also shared their opinion that they felt that some parents brought their children from Mexico to work rather than to attend school and that other parents felt that their children could drop out at age 16 since they were, in their eyes, adults and responsible enough to make such a decision. This was not the attitude of the parents involved in this research, yet the messages students received at home and the messages they received at school were not compatible. At home the message was to do well and graduate from high school, and at school, in honors classes, the message was to do well in order to prepare yourself for college. At school the message beginning in the freshman year was that high school was a blank slate where everyone could qualify for a college education, while at home the emphasis on being well-educated included being a good son/daughter and being able to respect and take care of your family.

While all of the students appeared to have successfully negotiated a smart academic identity, for at least one student this negotiation brought recognition that it was necessary to assimilate in order not to draw attention to himself in the classroom. Fidel explained:

> Yes, I assimilated into American culture because you have to.
> Well, it's because I am in honors classes and that makes all of
> my friends White except for one Hispanic guy and he speaks
> English all the time, he's not a Spanish speaker. Yes, I guess I
> have assimilated to American culture because I just don't want
> to stand out that much.

While all of the students maintained a strong Mexican transnational identity (speaking Spanish, being aware of current events in Mexico, respecting and enjoying cultural traditions of their families), it can also be argued that some level of forced assimilation was necessary for them to succeed in the academic classrooms at BGHS.

MASTER NARRATIVES AND MAJORITARIAN STORIES AROUND BEING "ILLEGAL"

While social science has confirmed that Mexican immigrants elicit more negative attitudes than other immigrant groups, including that they are innately inferior, more prone to crime, and less deserving of resources (Cornelius, 2002; Murillo, 2002; Suárez-Orozco & Suárez-Orozco, 2001), we know less about the effects of social mirroring (Suárez-Orozco, 2001) on young adults who experience prejudices and negative stereotypes.

"Illegal", and other pejorative labels, are what Solis (Solis 2002; Solis, 2004) defines as "narratives of rejection." Solis (2002) argues that when undocumented immigrants enter the United States, they are identified and must identify themselves according to the legal terms that are available to them. Therefore, she argues Mexican youth become undocumented immigrants as a "result of the conditions of poverty that force them out of their country and discriminatory U.S. immigration policies that draw them into new situations of prejudice and exploitation." (307) Solis notes that while "illegality" is the only available identity afforded to undocumented immigrants, some are able to reject and oppose that label because of their understanding of the circumstances that brought them to the United States (primarily economic). Ultimately, she argues, it is possible for undocumented immigrants to confront the narratives of rejection and to argue for their own human and legal rights. Her research showed that organizations in New York City like *Asociacion Tepeyac*[16] help define undocumented immigrants' "legitimacy" through the economic, social, and moral contributions they make to the U.S. society on a daily basis. Solis demonstrated how undocumented immigrant students move through a

---

[16] For more information on Asociacion Tepeyac and their work with the Mexican immigrant community in New York City see their website at http://www.tepeyac.org/

process of defining themselves as "undocumented" rather than "illegal" to obtain a positive but less common epistemological status.

Straddling two cultures of "smart academic identity" and "transnational cultural identity," the students also had to manage the grand narratives that label "illegal" aliens as less deserving and as lawbreaking (Murillo, 1997). Did the students interpolate the label and identity of "illegal", or like Solis' students (2002, 2004) did they see themselves as undocumented immigrants who because of circumstance were in a precarious position, but still were deserving of legal rights and privileges? All of the students, who graduated in the top 25 percent of their class (with the exception of one student) and made attempts to access higher education, constructed identities that allowed them to thrive in their varying worlds (school, home, and their life with peers and in the outside community). Still, was "illegal" an identity that they acknowledged or accepted?

SCHOOL ENVIRONMENT: SAFE SPACE OR DANGER ZONE?

Exploring the school environment in relationship to the students' documentation status is a more difficult task to outline. Some of the general answers I set out to discover were how the school treated undocumented students, the students' perceptions of how the school received them, and the reasons undocumented students stayed in high school if they knew that college was an unlikely future option.

Looking for these answers led me to recognize that BGHS undocumented students had multiple identities, practiced in multiple and shifting contexts. Sometimes students' multiple identities overlapped in places like the soccer field, where student athletes were encouraged to do well in school, to be proud of their cultural heritage, and to use their family work ethic in disciplining themselves for their sport. At other times their identities remained very separated: in their honors and AP courses, their academic identity was most valued, so students chose to hide their undocumented status for fear of reaction from white peers. Sometimes, sadly, when students would have preferred to practice only one identity, such as their smart academic identity when applying for college and working on scholarship applications, their undocumented identity impinged on their lived reality. Frances spoke of filling out applications and realizing that she would have to pay a different price because of her documentation status: "I read it in some of the college applications first. Like the information about being out-of-state or international. And when I read, it I was like 'dang it's a lot of money, that's like double!'" Different contexts required different identities. In some contexts, students chose which identity they wanted to practice; in other contexts, they were positioned into identities they did not choose; in still others, they were encouraged by teachers to incorporate multiple identities.

Teachers and students had varied reactions to the school's treatment of Latino students. On the positive side, the teachers argued that Benson Guthrie had worked harder each year to encourage more Latino students to join the honors and AP courses; consequently, their numbers in those courses had increased each year. At the same time the school's ESL program was an inclusion model where "newcomer" students were separated from their English-dominant classmates for six months to a year and then placed in mainstream courses where teachers felt ill-equipped or trained to make appropriate modifications for the immigrant students. Several of the teachers were impressed by the lack of racial tension in the school and generally believed that all of the different races got along quite well. However, while there may have been little physical fighting or signs of visible racial tension, Mr. John commented that Latino students

> Don't feel welcome and they don't feel connected to the school. Some of the kids are in sports, and I think one student might be involved in DECA. But these kids (before the soccer team was formed) were not participating in their school; they were not wearing the colors of their school. Even now I don't know if they feel like they are a part of the school.

It could also be argued that the school was taking steps in the right direction by hiring more Latino staff (including a high level administrator and a couple teachers) who could act as role models to the Latino student population. In addition to this, the school had a very successful Latino student group on campus that was created to "Be proud of being Hispanic and to do well and to graduate." Countering progress of adding a Latino student organization and a few Latino faculty members were the prejudices of different teachers in the school who one teacher ally admitted, felt, "Kids who are born here, they (other teachers) think they might be a better student. The ones that some teachers aren't sure about are the ones that haven't been here for long and don't speak very good English." That same teacher commented that certain subject departments in the school were more willing than others to work with new immigrant students. The teachers' reflections on the school environment were that school was a warm space, but, in some contexts, an alienating environment for Latino students.

Surprisingly, while the teacher allies had mixed feelings and were somewhat critical about the environment of the school, student participants shared more positive than negative feelings about how they were treated in the school. Students argued that the issue of being undocumented was relatively ignored and four of the five students said that they didn't feel they were treated any differently than their other classmates. Ricardo, for example remarked, "I don't really think they treat Hispanics or undocumented students differently. They [teachers] pretty much told me the same thing, just try hard, so that's what my idea was." Carmen said, "I think the teachers tell me not to get stuck where I am at, to finish high school and to keep on going, to keep up the good work and to keep being myself." Among the students, only Frances (arguably the most vocally critical of her schooling experience) admitted feeling that teachers did have lower expectations for Latino students and did not consider her "college material" because of her documentation status.

The students also felt that there were many teachers at the school who had encouraged them to do well in school and to try and continue their education. While not all of their teachers were aware of the students' documentation status, many were and continued to encourage them and to try and help them investigate ways to apply to colleges and to get scholarships that did not require legal residency. In addition to the teacher allies, the students mentioned other teachers, staff members, and coaches who had encouraged them to succeed.

The data support that the school was both a safe space for these "smart" undocumented Latino students as well as a danger zone where both the structures of the school system (an immersion ESL program, a system that placed newcomers back in the ninth grade regardless of their grade level in their country of origin) and the negative beliefs toward *some* Latino students created mixed messages and experiences for different types of Latino students at BGHS. The data support that these students were able to use their "smart student" identity to favorably position themselves in the school environment. All of the students who had excelled since their arrival in Sunder Crossings were able to maneuver themselves into positions of success at school, which allowed them to pass through the educational pipeline up until they made attempts to access the college pipeline. At the moment they tried to access the college pipeline, they came up against the concrete barriers of the policies and laws that relegated them to a second-class citizenship, as "illegal immigrants".

The paradox of the school environment was that students did not confront the issue of being "illegal" until they began the college application process or began making post-high school plans, because at BGHS, the issues of their being undocumented residents was invisible and ignored. Yet, while we know that invisibility can be both protective and destructive (Brayboy, 2004), their invisibility in this case was not crafted by public sentiment but by laws that forbade teachers to ask them whether or not they were undocumented or schools to collect data regarding on whether or not students were undocumented.

The federal law that made it illegal for faculty and staff members to ask children about their citizenship status was created as a way to protect them from any discrimination that might result. One teacher emphasized the difficulties caused by the law:

> You have to take it into consideration that we can't ask whether or not a student is undocumented. It's not really fair, though, because you can't really help them or give them an honest answer to their questions. Legally, you are not supposed to be talking about them being undocumented.

While many of the teacher allies had developed trusting relationship with their students, and students had offered this information about themselves on their own, other teachers had found legitimate reasons to ask students about their status (for the purpose of college application or applying to special programs at the school). One teacher commented that when she was trying to help students with their college applications, she would explain to them that

> If they are a resident and a citizen of the United States and have lived in North Carolina for at least five years then they are considered in-state, and then I say if you're not a citizen or current resident of North Carolina then you are considered out-of-state, even though you have lived in North Carolina for maybe four or five years. I guess I'm sort of asking them if

they're documented or undocumented, but I sort of find a way
to go around it.

While the teacher allies found it frustrating to be technically unable to talk about students' documentation status, especially when helping them apply to college, they also realized that this law was created to protect the students. Mr. David, who was glad that the issue could not be discussed openly in school, argued, " There is enough stigma attached to being an ESL student, and the stigma of being an undocumented student would be a further division, not just by race, but documented and undocumented. While it complicates it by making it unknown, it may create more stigmas if people knew."   So while undocumented students were legal, in the sense that they had a right to attend K-12 school, they were not legally allowed to continue on to college without paying as though they were international or out-of-state students. For these undocumented students, the college application process was the first act that publicly signaled their status.

UNDOCUMENTED AND UNABLE TO CONTINUE: WHAT NOW?

While the school was not allowed to talk about it (officially), the students, as well as many of their peers, all became aware at some point in high school that they would not be able to continue on to college. They discovered that some universities would not admit undocumented students, and that universities in North Carolina which admit undocumented students required them to pay out-of-state tuition. As Suárez-Orozco and Suárez-Orozco (2001) emphasize, even though the US Supreme Court Case *Plyer v. Doe* (1982) protects the rights of undocumented minors to attend public school, it is not hard to envision the many ways lack of legal status could be disruptive to a student's United States school experience. Thus, the most compelling question regarding these students is why they remain in school at all?

Their teachers provided varying justifications and reasons for the undocumented students to remain in their classes. The majority of the teacher allies agreed that for many students' families, graduating from high school is in itself a major accomplishment and fulfills their expectation; thus, the children remain in school. Teacher Mr. Carlos agreed: "For most of the kids, they are going to be the first one in their family to graduate from high school, and that's an achievement in itself. Without seeing further beyond to them and their families, without seeing further beyond high school, graduation is a very big deal in many of their families." This reasoning suggests a form of resistance that displays a transformative rationale (Yosso, 2006), wherein the parents and the children recognize that despite not having access to a college education, a high school diploma is a form of knowledge that they can receive and that cannot be taken away from them. The support and encouragement of family is a major reason that teachers believe undocumented students remain in school.

Many teachers also believed that their undocumented students were bright and intrinsically motivated, and therefore genuinely enjoyed being in school. Ms. Jennifer who had had many new immigrant students in her classroom commented,

> So sometimes you don't have family encouraging you and it's just an intrinsic motivation, like Maria (a pseudonym). She was one of the most motivated students I've ever taught. It was all coming from herself, and it didn't even seem to be an element of competitiveness. She didn't ever look around to see what the others were doing, she was so motivated for herself.

Teachers also mentioned that many of the bright and motivated undocumented students influenced their classmates to work hard as well. These kids, who were described as "hard workers" and "real intellectuals," encouraged their Latino classmates by their examples to continue to work hard and stay in school despite undocumented status. The teachers also believed that staying in school was a rational decision for many undocumented students. Several teachers commented that staying in high school to learn English was economically a smart move for future work. As Mr. David explained:

> You can earn $12 per hour in the chicken plant if you have good English. You only get an $8 per hour job if you don't speak good English or no English. And I'm not saying that that's the entire motivation for all of them, but it definitely doesn't hurt.

Learning English, he noted, also meant an opportunity to achieve a higher-level management position rather than a lower-level position:

"If you learn English well enough, then you're not going to be on the chain gang, you're going to be one of the bosses, and that's the expectation (from families)." Several of the teachers also mentioned students who officially dropped out but returned in order to hold adult responsibilities at bay, to spend time with their friends, and to play soccer for the high school. One teacher remarked that undocumented students were keenly aware of how American's society was structured: "They know that more education may equal more money than they can make without a diploma." Thus, while dropping out was one decision that many undocumented students had made long before graduation day, the decision to remain was often made for the personal and economic benefit to the undocumented students and their families.

For their part, the students who had developed a strong academic identity, appeared more prone to remain because of this identity. Researchers note that the immigrant students who are most likely to succeed are those who arrive with an academic foundation, particularly if they are fully literate in their primary language (Suárez-Orozco & Suárez-Orozco, 2001). Arguably all five of the students arrived in Sunder Crossings with just such an academic foundation and with an already established "smart identity" from their schools in Mexico. This "smart identity" was nurtured and encouraged by their teachers in both countries and helped them continue on in high school despite their undocumented status. Students without this "smart identity" were likely to be positioned differently in school.

For an extremely academically focused student such as the school's academic superstar, Fidel, remaining in school also meant holding on to hope that the laws could change and gaining as much education as possible in the meantime. Fidel commented,

> You know, I do know why I take AP classes. It is because, when I found out I was not going to be able to go to college, I sort of got very depressed. Well, then I found out that these courses could give me college credit and then I thought well maybe that is the closest I am going to get to college, I mean a real college class and that's why I work hard. Last year I was under the notion that I was never going to go to college, so I thought that this is the closest I am ever going to get, so I'll just do it.

Several of the students held out hope that things would change, even through the spring of their senior year. While some students such as Frances did not see the need to talk about the undocumented issue because, "It doesn't make a difference between us [those who are undocumented]. Why would we talk about it, because it's not going to make a big difference?" Others were more willing to discuss feeling betrayed by the system. Two of the students openly admitted that they did not work as hard once they realized it was unlikely that they would be continuing on to college. While Saul tried to hold out hope that his situation might be different, the reality of what happens to undocumented students each year after graduation eventually wore him down:

> Then my sophomore year I started reconsidering and I thought maybe those students just messed up. Maybe they were just like troublemakers. So I was thinking that maybe I can still make it to college. But after my sophomore year, the next generation of students finished and the same thing happened (no one went to college). Except for Sophia and she was the only one who got into college, but she had documentation. The same thing happened with the rest of people.

By the spring of his senior year, after he had not been accepted at his top choice university, Saul admitted:

> I didn't really think it was important anymore, because the years kept coming, and nobody got to go to college. So, I applied to University X, but I got turned down and I knew that I was going to get turned down because of the way that I had done my junior year and my senior year. I just did it [applied] so that people couldn't say that I didn't try. And right now I'm a senior and I'm not really thinking about going to college anymore. Not right now, at least. I probably might go in like a couple years, but for right now I've decided what I need to do is work.

While Saul did not drop out, he did confess that knowing he was undocumented had affected the effort that he put forth in his classes.

This was also the case for other students. Carmen's grades had not dropped significantly by the end of her senior year, but she had dropped her position of President of the Latino student organization and was taking on more and more hours at her "part-time" job. By the end of his senior year, Ricardo, who was facing possible legal problems because of his problems with a fake social security card, became angry and hopeless regarding his situation and, despite having a strong academic record, did not even consider completing his college applications. Ultimately, Ricardo said, " I thought about it and then I looked into the possibilities, and I realized that there was no way, and then I got upset for a while, and right now I'm at a point where I don't really care."

SCHOOL BOTH A SAFE SPACE AND DANGER ZONE

Historically, scholars have argued that schools are places where the status quo is maintained and that children learn their place in a hierarchy that is socially and economically stratified (Bowles and Gintis, 1976). Scholars have also argued that schools indoctrinate students into assimilationist practices that poorly match up with world views of students who are "different" than the white Anglo-Saxon mainstream (Gonzalez, 1990; San Miguel; 1987, Reese, 1996). For transnational students, especially for the Mexican-American students, this case has been argued with convincing evidence from their lived experiences (Valenzuela, 1999). While I was prepared to find that BGHS was a site of multiple oppressions, given that school can be an alienating experience for Mexican immigrants, I was surprised to find that school was also a safe space that protected these children from an "illegal" reality. More important, these children protected themselves by using their "smart" academic identity to position themselves positively at school.

The school was a protective space because legal policies kept teachers from asking questions about citizenship status and created invisibility for these students. At the same time, it did not prepare undocumented students for real life after high school. While history has rarely demonstrated that conventional institutions such as school would ever be "allowed" to become an advocacy/activist space for students of color, and rarely have served such a function, BGHS remains a safe space that, nevertheless underserves all of its undocumented students by remaining silent and/or ignoring the role played by documentation status after high school graduation.

CROSSING OVER: LIFE AFTER HIGH SCHOOL

> In this community, first let's talk about within the school because within the school is different from the community as a whole. I really don't know anybody here (in the school) who is not heartbroken, at least the adults in this building, by the situation when we see exceptional young people are not having an opportunity. – Ms. Olivia

> Once they graduate they have to enter into this world, and I think some of them are smart enough to realize that, "I gotta think like an undocumented person now and I need to come up with a fake name, a fake ID and pay for those things to get my job." –Mr. John

The students' "undocumented" identity (Solis, 2002; Solis,2004) is transformed to "illegal" status" after students in Sunder Crossings leave the safe space of the high school. While students began experiencing the confines of both illegal and undocumented identities as they attempted to prepare for a life after high school --one they hoped would include college-- they did not fully experience or adopt this additional undocumented/illegal identity in high school.

> I don't know, it's kind of like a song that I play; it says I am not from over there and I am not from here. I guess you could say I am a boy without a country.—Ricardo

This quote illuminates the change that occurs when the undocumented students graduated from high school and begin their lives as adults, and also highlights the emotions a broken immigration system creates. After graduation the protective space of the school evaporates, and the world where students must figure out how to live without "papers" begins.

Graduation from high school signals a significant shift in context; for many undocumented students, life as illegal workers begins. Yet, most of the BGHS students like those in Solis' research (Solis, 2001; Solis, 2004; Solis, 2005), began, and in many cases, continued to construct their identities as "undocumented" rather than "illegal" persons. While Fidel was the only student able to continue on to a four-year university, the majority of the other students lived their lives with dignity and pride, and saw their immediate futures as counternarratives to the narratives of rejection that had been crafted in mainstream media about "illegal immigrants".

While I have outlined the obstacles that exist for college-ready undocumented students, the data collected throughout their senior year (and for several of them through the fall of their first year after high school) showed that the students understood that their future life trajectories would interpolate them as both "undocumented" and "illegal." While school and the students' "smart" identity protected them from an "illegal" identity to a point, during the end of high school they began to craft their identities and to consider what an "illegal" versus "undocumented" future meant for each of them, especially when they faced the college application process.

In my interviews with the students, we discussed friends and classmates who had graduated and who also were undocumented students. During our conversations, we discussed whether they knew any students who had been able to go on to college and, if not, what they did after graduation. Every student noted that working at the local poultry plant or at a fast food restaurant was an option many of their former classmates followed. Frances commented, "All the people I know that are undocumented are working at places like McDonalds." However, these students hoped not to have to pursue those occupations after graduation. Many of them said they saw themselves differently than their counterparts who went to work in the factory after high school. Carmen insisted,

> I don't want to be like every Hispanic student, spend all four years to only like go to work at a chicken factory or somewhere else. There are some students that are like really, really smart and they finish high school, and they just go to work at McDonald's or the chicken plant. I want to keep going because I don't want to end up like them. My family makes a big difference.

Saul also rejected these limited options:

> I have decided that I'm leaving and I'm not going to stay in Sunder Crossings. You know, I didn't know if you knew, but I quit my position at Wendy's. I told them that I was not

interested in training as an assistant manager. I just told them that I didn't see myself in the long-term working as a manager at a fast food restaurant.

When the students spoke of jobs in the chicken factory or fast food, they emphasized that students who worked in those positions after high school had given up on having any other choice about their future. The students' feelings toward working in these places was not of shame (many of them had parents who worked in these places) but of loss of hope that they would be able to make their decisions for the future for themselves. Carmen commented with sadness, "They (other undocumented Latinos) just say it's their destiny, because they don't have a choice as to where they go. They say that if they really wanted to finish high school or go to college somewhere, they can't do it, so that's where they are going." While many of the student participants were not optimistic about college plans, they were hopeful that they would have a more active choice about their lives than their peers after high school.

The teacher allies also understood the difference between the "undocumented" versus "illegal" identity. Their encouragement towards higher education or other skilled jobs upon graduation signaled an attempt to position the kids to craft "undocumented" identities. While all of the teacher allies had encouraged students to pursue higher education, by helping them fill out applications, making phone calls to universities on behalf of their students, writing letters of recommendation for them, and taking them on trips to visit universities, the teachers also were critical of the school's inability to encourage alternative options to college. While teachers recognized the danger that occurred if a student were to be caught with a fake ID or fake papers, they still felt that the school could be doing more to encourage students into skilled trade occupations, since paying for out-of-state tuition was going to be a financial impossibility for nearly all of the undocumented students at BGHS. Mr. Carlos tried to identify to his students what other opportunities existed:

> I don't tell them that college is not the only option. I show them different options like going to community college or the fact that they could be a good mechanic, or the fact that they could be a good cook or chef. I can't say that college is the only option for them, because if I say that and they're just

going to be frustrated, because we know that not all of them
will go to college. So I think it's important for them to know
that there are other things that they can do like a carpenter or
mechanic or different things.

Saul also mentioned that the school could do a better job encouraging
undocumented students into different fields, because 4-year college was
not going to be a practical choice for many of them.

I think that they could be encouraging other job opportunities.
Like for example drafting-- they have a class in drafting and
it's actually a really good class. And it teaches you how to
read construction plans and everything. It's important to offer
options for people that might not be going to college. They
should be teaching people about the kind of job you can get if
you don't go to college. They should be giving students
different skills that they could use if they don't go to college.

In addition to recognizing that going on to college or working in more
high-skilled jobs would create better economic opportunities for
undocumented students, the teachers recognized that the jobs where
students did not have to report income might be easily available for the
students, yet that these same jobs would likely be unfulfilling. Low-
level jobs which would be readily available for "illegal" workers were
not the types of opportunities they envisioned for these students'
futures. Ms. Stacey mentioned that, although she preferred not to,
when all other options had failed she would, "Sometimes even suggest
that they try to find work where they are not going to have to report
their income. You know, like if you can clean houses in your
neighborhood, or maybe go to another neighborhood to clean houses,
or mow lawns for cash, things of that nature."

While no one intended to imply that people who work low-wage or
entry-level jobs are less capable or less worthy, all the students, the
teacher allies and the researcher recognized that self-fulfillment in these
positions is limited. The students and teachers also seemed to recognize
that people in these positions are named, labeled, and positioned as
"illegal." The difference in the undocumented student participants and
their undocumented classmates, who may have accepted the "illegal"
life as their destiny, appeared to be that their "smart" identity in school

not only protected them but also created some level of the hope that their lives could be different than those that came before them.

THE LIVED FUTURE AFTER HIGH SCHOOL

By graduation day the future of each of the undocumented students had begun to play itself out in identities that I interpreted as "undocumented," "illegal," and "legal." As they walked across the stage with their diplomas, their contexts and identities inevitably began to change. The identities they had negotiated during high school, which included a "smart" academic identity, a transnational identity, and at times an undocumented identity, now began to shift. This period of identity re-construction included both conceptual and procedural processes (Holland et al. 1998), where students were not only articulating their legal status in different ways but also acted in the world in an embodiment of both "illegal" and "undocumented" identities. Less than six months after they graduated from high school, their "undocumented" versus "illegal" identity was still being constructed.

For one student, Fidel, the future began at a four-year university on a full tuition, room and board, four-year scholarship. Up to this point no undocumented student at his high school had been able to do so, but Fidel successfully applied, was accepted, and found funding for his college dream. While the obstacles of being an undocumented student created multiple difficulties in starting at the university, Fidel negotiated the terrain with multiple tactics and a great amount of humility and grace. While still fearful of other students' reactions to his immigration status, Fidel participates in the Latino student organization on his campus, which fights for more educational equality for Latino students, including the passage of the federal DREAM Act. Fidel admitted that while he is grateful to be at university, he also feels somewhat alienated because he is the only undocumented student on campus. At BGHS he had at least been in the company of many other students and friends who shared his documentation status.

The two women in the study, Carmen and Frances, were accepted at two different private universities, and Frances received a private scholarship that would have allowed her to continue her education. Carmen, on the other hand, received a small scholarship, but it was not enough to pay for the high tuition at a private, Catholic university.

Frances's extended family members who are legal permanent residents, hoped to adopt her, so they sent her back to Mexico while they completed the paperwork for her adoption. The most critical of all the students, by the fall of 2006 Frances had not returned from Mexico and her brother was unaware of if and when she would return. Frances returned to Mexico as a legal citizen of that country. Carmen continued to work at her fast food job, and hoped to take some courses at the local community college in the spring. Despite her inability to attend a four-year university, she remained positive that she would find a way to attend university.

Saul, the eloquent young man with the highly supportive family, was not accepted to the one university to which he applied and had decided to take a job after high school that would provide a steady income to help out his family. While Saul was disappointed that he had not been accepted at the competitive university, he commented, "I strongly believe that college is not the only place that you can learn, and I want to be able to prove that to myself. Hopefully I will be able to do that for myself." In addition, Saul felt his new job as a welder would allow him opportunities to fulfill dreams he had:

> I'm planning to leave and work with a friend who is currently working as a welder. I think, you know, that it's really a pretty good job. The job means that I will actually move around. He is currently in Asheville, but the job moves somewhere different every few months. The job means traveling all around the United States, which is the part that I like the most. And I have always dreamed about traveling around the United States. He said it's really an advantage because I speak such good English. And now I just need to learn how to weld, and I will go to Florida to train for how to do that.

Saul was proud to have a job that would allow him to send money back to his family, to demonstrate his work ethic, and to see new places outside Sunder Crossings.

The final student, Ricardo, had become frustrated by the laws and policies in the United States, and ultimately decided that applying to college was a "waste of his time." His hopelessness was aggravated by his mounting legal problems over the false identity charges that had been brought against him. Following my final interview with Ricardo, I never saw or spoke with him again. One teacher told me that another student had seen him around Sunder Crossings after graduation but that he didn't appear to be working. Another teacher ran into him in town and said he looked like he had lost a great amount of weight and didn't seem to be doing very well. While the teachers encouraged him to keep in touch, by the late fall of 2006, no one at the school had seen him for quite some time; some students had heard that he moved away from Sunder Crossings. Most likely, his mounting legal problems encouraged his disappearance and increasing invisibility in the community.

While each of these students navigated multiple identities in school, all were beginning to negotiate new terrain, the shift from school to life after high school marked a significant identity construction period. For four of the students (Fidel, Saul, Frances and Carmen), this shift included choices that moved them toward an "undocumented" identity which justified their status in the country in terms of "human rights and social justice" (Solis, 2001) and helped them create counternarratives to the label of "illegal" or "other." Frances was unique in that her departure to Mexico reaffirmed her "transnational cultural identity" and possibly de-emphasized or eliminated her "undocumented" status. Ricardo, however, appeared to be moving toward an "illegal" life that, even before the research concluded, was being lived in the shadows of increased marginalization.

The multiple identities of the undocumented students and the effects these identities played on their lived futures brings into question the role the school should play in giving the undocumented students tools to live and thrive (even survive) after high school. While it is not surprising that the conventional institution of school was not a site for advocacy for these students, school was a safe space where these students felt protected. If spaces in school are not willing to take it one step further, such as the after-school Latino student club, and create the same type of environment that non-profits such as *Tepeyac* in New York City have created, students may have to rely on their homes and outside organizations in the community to serve this role. The ongoing struggle for social justice and praxis to which CRT and LatCrit subscribe obliges us to consider these difficult issues. Activism for these students' human rights, both as they negotiate school and as they cross over into their "undocumented" and "illegal" futures, must come from within their own community and from those people who have institutional power and the legalized status to fight the battle with them.

CHAPTER 7

Tactics of Resistance for Undocumented, Mexican Origin Students

When Fidel got back to school this year he came by during one of our workdays, and I would start to talk back to him, do you have your list of the schools that you are going to apply to and so and so, and I asked him if he was working on his essays, because we had talked about that last spring, and he says to me, "I have a little problem." And this is what we continue to refer to it as, as a little problem. And I looked at him and I said, "Oh no," and he looked back at me and said, "Oh yeah," and I knew immediately that he was undocumented. And I was just sick because a lot of students are in this situation, you know, but this was the first time that he felt comfortable, and I guess he decided that he might as well, this was the time to tell us, because we were going to find out anyway during the college process...

> I have to tell you that fighting this process is not only a challenge for our Latino students, but to every student who has not had a parent go through college. It became fairly clear to Fidel all along the way that he was going to apply to some other places other than University X, but because there were people at University X, who made it a priority to look carefully at students who are in his situation and to make it less of a barrier than a lot of other schools, he realized that University X was going to be his best chance…

> Because if there's anybody that I know that has coping skills, and strategy skills, this is not somebody who has had everything done for them their whole lives, this is a child who better than anybody else in his class looks down the road, and anticipates what am I going to need in order to get things done, because he has had to do that his whole life and he has not had a choice. And in that sense he is like an adult, and his classmates are still kids. So he can do that, and I really don't have, well the first month or two (of college) will really be rough, because it will be overwhelming. But once he passes that…

In the above account Ms. Olivia, a teacher ally, described the tactics that Fidel employed during his senior year of high school, and through the process of applying to college as an undocumented student. Such tactics, often practiced within the confines of the school system and the application process, were much like what de Certau (1984) calls those tactics employed by the "weak" in order to take advantage of the moments when those in power have a lapse of control. While Fidel's tactics demonstrate one way that students' resist within and against the system, this chapter examines the multiple ways that undocumented students practiced strategies of resistance within their educational trajectories.

The theoretical constructs of domination, resistance and agency provide a useful lens through which to view the students and how they have responded to the multiple obstacles placed in front of them. While Scott (1990) emphasized that resistance is often practiced behind closed doors, through "hidden transcripts," de Certau argued that tactics of resistance may be practiced upon the terrain of those in power, in even more subtle ways that may not be as "visible" as a public performance or as veiled as a "hidden transcript".

LatCrit scholars Dolores Delgado-Bernal (Delgado-Bernal, 1998; Delgado-Bernal, 2001), Daniel Solórzano (Solórzano & Delgado-Bernal, 2001; Solórzano & Yosso, 2001), and Tara Yosso (Solórzano & Yosso, 2001; Yosso, 2006) expanded the possibilities of where resistance is practiced by Latino students, arguing that resistance manifests itself in varying categories and behaviors. These categories can include both internal (more subtle and covert forms of resistance) and external (more outward and visible critiques of the system). Students can also display varying levels of opposition including reactionary, self-defeating, conformist, transformational, and resilient resistance. These varying forms of resistance were apparent in the behaviors of the five undocumented students as they negotiated their senior year of high school and their post-high school plans.

While these undocumented Latino students practiced strategies of resistance as they navigated the educational pipeline, they each did so in various forms. For some, the public performance and the hidden transcript varied dramatically, for they chose to practice their resistance in more covert behaviors. For other students, a more public and outward resistance was displayed in their actions. These students, as de Certau (1984) suggests, practiced their tactics of resistance by utilizing the "cracks" in the higher education system where they found moments to change the system, even if ever so slightly. It is also important to keep in mind that the students existed in a liminal space that places them betwixt and between being American or Mexican and being a lawbreaker and high-achiever. Resistance does not occur along one established continuum: "Chicano students live between and within the layers of subordination, based on race, class, gender, language, immigration status, accent and phenotype so that these students do not "fit" neatly into one single category of consciousness and/or forms of resistance." (Solórzano and Yosso, 2002, p.162)

OBSTACLES

Just as current policies do not create any level of access or opportunity for higher education among undocumented Latino students, multiple obstacles further lessen their opportunities. The more concrete obstacles witnessed included lack of citizenship, language barriers, differing expectations between family and school, job responsibilities, and money problems. The difficulties of being a Latino student who was not considered "college material," who arrived late to high school, and who was not able to amass enough honors and AP coursework to be competitive at more selective four-year institutions, and who faced low expectations from the school system administrators ("oh, you won't find any undocumented students who are capable of doing college work") underlie their schooling experiences.

In addition to these daily struggles, as students began the college application process, they were faced with a lack of access to in-state tuition, a requirement to apply as and to compete in the out-of-state student pool, a lack of access to scholarships which were reserved for citizens and legal permanent residents, and the difficulty of filling out an application as an "out-of-state student/international student". One student remarked, "It was difficult because I had to send in a different form about not applying for an I-9 Visa, so I had to apply as an out-of-state student and I could not answer some of the questions. They also wanted information on financial stuff that I could not fill out because I don't have any money and neither does my family."

While the multiple obstacles stood in the way and constrained their possibilities, undocumented students employed innovative tactics of resistance against such obstacles. While self-defeating resistance (Willis, 1977) sometimes occurred, stronger forms of resistance existed and thrived, offering the hope that a transformative experience is possible.

GENERAL TACTICS OF RESISTANCE IN THE HIGH SCHOOL

The tactics which the students used within their daily experiences in the high school were done so under the constraints of a highly structured public school system. Murillo's research (2002) in Sunder Crossings showed the school system created a type of "Mexican-typed" schooling that mirrored the "Mexican-typed" jobs given to Latinos working in the poultry plants in the community. Both the school and the community have grown to become more inclusive toward the Latino community since Murillo's time in Sunder Crossings, yet the undocumented students still felt as though acting "American" (white) was the best way to navigate the system. Fidel remarked, "As a way to fit in, I assimilate into American culture because you have to, because I am in honors classes and all my friends are white expect for one Hispanic guy who speaks English all the time, he's not a Spanish speaker. Yeah, I guess I've assimilated to American culture because I just don't want to stand out that much." Other students mentioned that learning and speaking English well was another way to create success for themselves. Carmen said, "I had, like, three or four dictionaries at home, and if I heard a word that I didn't know I would just like write it down and then every night I would look it up in the dictionary. I had no choice, I had to do this to learn to communicate effectively with others." While numerous authors argue that assimilation has negative effects on immigrant children (Portes & Rumbaut, 2001; Suárez-Orozco & Suárez-Orozco, 2000; Valdez, 1996), these students used conformist resistance to achieve success in their school system.

Other students displayed more public performances of resistance to the system. In the case of Frances, a student who moved between the United States and Mexico multiple times and therefore had strong English skills, the school tried to place her back in ninth grade even though she had transcripts from Mexico to prove that she should be given enough credits to start school as a junior. Frances and her uncle fought this placement, as she explained in her interview with me:

> Frances: I just got them (transcripts) off the Internet, because I went to high school in Mexico City at a high school that was part of UNAM (large university in Mexico City). And so from the web site you could, like, download your grades or whatever. So, like, at the beginning every newcomer at Benson Guthrie, they would always put them as freshmen, no matter how much English, they seemed to know and I mean that's not bad, for students who need to learn English, but I didn't need to learn English. So, in the beginning I was in all these ESL classes, and I didn't need them.

> Janet: So did one of your teachers figure out that you knew English really well?

> Frances: I don't know, I guess they just originally put me as a freshman and then I took another test and I did well, and then I brought my grades in and I asked them if they were going to count them and they were, like, "no we can't," and I to kept asking them, "why not?" They told me originally that they would take them as elective credits, and I just kept coming back every day. And my uncle would come back every day asking them why they wouldn't accept the credits, and then finally at the end they were like, "yeah okay, whatever, we'll count them." So I went from being a freshman to being a junior.

> Janet: So, it sounds like your uncle knew the school system well enough to come in and advocate for you.

> Frances: Yeah, that too, but I mean, I think they just finally got tired of me. So they let me in to the junior classes, they got tired of me going there every day and bothering them. And I think, like I really think, they don't expect us to go to college, so they just think well this girl just wants to graduate from high school. So just give her the credits, so she can get done with school.

> Janet: So you think that they don't have high expectations for all students. For students that aren't citizens?

> Frances: No, like, some other teachers do, like Ms. Stacey or Ms. Olivia. I guess most teachers know that we don't have the documents, so they don't think we can get in to college.

Not only did Frances's uncle, who had lived a while in the United States and was now a legal permanent resident, possess the cultural capital (Bourdieu, 1986; Stanton-Salazar, 1995; Stanton-Salazar & Spina, 2000; Stanton-Salazar & Spina, 2003) to understand that parents could visit the counselors and argue for their student's rights, but Frances herself also actively approached the counselors and argued on her own. Rather than remaining complicit in her grade placement, she found a way to be placed in the appropriate grade level. Working within the constraints of the school system's policy for "newcomers," Frances was able to change the course of her future at Benson Guthrie High School.

SPECIFIC COLLEGE TACTICS

These students also had to consider tactics that would be necessary for navigating their way to college as undocumented students in North Carolina. Their interviews revealed that they had devised numerous tactics to challenge the policies that prohibited them from attending college in North Carolina as in-state residents. Many of these ideas, which were kept to private conversations among the students and their friends and family, or even between me and the student, could be considered hidden transcripts (Scott, 1990) that were occurring "offstage" from public discourse at Benson Guthrie. These hidden transcripts were criticisms against the laws that prohibited them from being seen as North Carolina residents.

> I think we are all humans and if we have the capacity to continue in school we should be able to do so. That's really hard. I think like if that person really wants to, say, be somebody in the future, it doesn't matter if they are illegal or not they should have the same opportunities because I think that everybody that wants to do it should be able to finish their education. --Carmen

> I think I would tell them that if you do want to and get to go to college, that is a sign that you will be a productive member of society in some way. --Ricardo

> I didn't really want to go to college just to make more money. I guess I wanted to get into college, just to see what college life was like. I want to experience different things and learn about different things in life. I think we should have access to that if it's what we want and we have worked for it. -- Saul

While students argued that the state should create an in-state tuition policy for undocumented students, they thought of ways they could accomplish their goals within the structures of the current policies. One of the primary tactics students considered was finding ways to become legal permanent residents. Frances, a student whose parents had passed away, and whose uncle and aunt were in the process of adopting her, saw legal permanent residency status as her ticket to college. Other students had a well developed understanding of immigration law and knew that if they had a job skill that the United States needed, they might be able to gain legal permanent residency through a work visa. Two students mentioned that becoming a nurse was a profession that might help them receive a work visa to remain in the United States.

As students who were unlikely able to gain legal permanent residency in the United States, at least in the foreseeable future, most students considered working under North Carolina's current policies by first attending a community college and then transferring to a four-year university. Four out of the five students said that although it would be a severe financial burden for them and their families, they would pay out-of-state tuition at a community college (around $3,000). They hoped that the laws would have changed by the time they could transfer to a four-year university.

At the same time, many students mentioned that while their families might be able to make a financial sacrifice to pay for community college, they would never ask them to do so. Saul said,

> I believe that I probably could make enough money to pay for that [community college], but that would be money that would be just for me and I couldn't spend all that money just on me. It has to go to my family and to my father. It would really be impossible right now.

This example also illustrates the cultural identity differences among Mexican-origin and American children which were discussed in earlier chapters.

Other tactics employed by these students included applying for scholarships which did not require American citizenship or legal permanent residency as a condition for application.[17] In North Carolina, unfortunately, only one scholarship like this existed.[18] Finally, some students considered returning to Mexico, starting college there, and returning to the United States in the future if residency rules had changed. To this end, Carmen, the student who had best maintained her academic competency in Spanish, had already researched what colleges were near her hometown in Mexico, how much tuition each of them charged, and what college entrance exams each required. BGHS did not actively help undocumented students pursue these "alternative" college options, so the students took it upon themselves to consider the ways that they achieve higher education despite the policies blocking

---

[17] For scholarships that do not require US citizenship as a requirement please see http://maldef.org/leadership/scholarships/general/.

[18] For scholarships that do not require US citizenship or North Carolina residency please see the North Carolina Society for Hispanic Professionals at http://www.thencshp.org/.

access to it.[19] In this way, the students practiced practical resistance toward a system that worked to exclude them.

SELF-DEFEATING RESISTANCE

In their study on transformative resistance, Solórzano and Delgado-Bernal (2001) noted that research on the theoretical concept of resistance has focused almost exclusively on the concept of self-defeating resistance (Fine, 1990; McClaren, 1993; Willis, 1977). In this type of resistance students make critiques of the system and act on those critiques, but ultimately those acts implicate them in reproducing oppressive conditions. In *Learning to Labor,* his classic study of social reproduction, Paul Willis (1977) demonstrates how the lads' behavior in school reproduced a working class culture, and ultimately guaranteed a working class future for each young man. While self-defeating resistance was not the only type of resistance that was practiced at Benson Guthrie, dropping out of school as a critique on the system was clearly a form of self-defeating resistance with the undocumented Latino student population.

In each of the interviews, I asked the students if they knew other people in their senior class who were in the same situation as themselves (undocumented and college ready). Each time I did this, the students would name the other four students participating in the research project and then indicate that many students who were in their same situation had dropped out of school, or had decided to take "easy" classes in order to finish high school without having to exert much effort. Ricardo mentioned, "There was another guy (in his honors classes) but when he figured things out he was like, "I'm not going to deal with that. Why create any extra work for myself? Why bother?" That makes things a lot harder, and it can just be easy and just finish out happy and go get a job."

In the Latino Outreach program I directed at the school, the inaugural class of sophomore students included five undocumented students, who had all been identified as high-achieving. By their senior year, the program's inaugural class had dwindled down to two students; the only legal permanent residents among them. Of those five students, two had dropped out of high school altogether before their senior years

---

[19] While individual teachers worked to help students with possible college options, the school system itself did not create programs that helped students who were undocumented.

and the other three had either lost interest in the program or rationalized that the amount of time and effort that was necessary to be an active member of the program was not worth the returns they would gain in the end.   One student, who had the responsibility of working after school at a box company and babysitting his siblings at home on the weekends, emailed me to apologize for dropping out.   More importantly, he wanted to inform me that he could not attend college in the United States, and that his family obligations were more important than being involved in the program. These students were all making a rational decision, yet ultimately their behavior --should laws change in North Carolina-- will harm their chances for accessing higher education.

All of the students also mentioned friends, family members, and classmates who dropped out of high school because there seemed to be no point to receiving a high school diploma without the opportunity to attend college. Once again, their rationale that one could start working and making money at 14 or 15 rather than at 18 showed judgment, yet,was ultimately a self-defeating behavior.   The words of Saul eloquently capture this behavior:

> Yes, a lot of my friends have dropped out. They started work right away, and they always give me a hard time like, "What are you doing man; you're just going to work at the poultry plant. You should just come start making money." I would talk to them and I would argue with them and say if you'd stayed in school you might be able to go to college. I tell them, watch me, I'm going to start college. And now they laughed at me because I'm not going to be able to do. They say, I told you so.

While Saul completed high school, ultimately he did not attend college directly after high school, so by the end of the research he had also begun to wonder if the tactic his friends had practiced was equally as useful as the one he had employed.

TRANSFORMATIVE RESISTANCE

There were also undocumented students at BGHS who not only criticized the conditions of undocumented students but also took active steps to change those conditions. These students were critical of the public school system, of immigration policy in the United States, and of the cultural norms held by U.S. society. While their practices varied,

I was consistently amazed by the potential these students displayed in being agents for change in their community. For example, during the spring of the students' senior year, an immigration rally was held in their community in response to the immigration legislation being proposed in Washington D.C. which would have started a series of Draconian laws against undocumented immigrants living in the United States. Ironically, the peaceful rally which occurred in Sunder Crossings took place on the very same site where only 10 years before a white supremacist group had held a rally to have all "illegal aliens" deported.

As an undocumented student living in a small community, marching in the rally and publicly "outing" herself was a dramatic and brave show of external resistance for Frances. In the days leading up to the rally she had been gathering support for the event inside the school, and speaking about issues concerning the DREAM Act on a local radio show hosted by a Hispanic community organization in town. She passed out fliers and led the group of students who marched from the high school to the rally downtown. In my fieldnotes I recalled, "While I was at the rally, I saw several of my participants and their families, and as different individuals of the Sunder Crossings community got up to give their speeches, I saw Frances stand up with a student group who collectively gave a passionate speech about the DREAM Act and letting undocumented students go to college. She had told me earlier in the week that they hoped to get 100 people to attend the rally, yet here were more than 6,000 people who had come to march peacefully and in solidarity for immigrant rights." This action Frances participated in displayed an open and visible declaration of resistance against the current policies concerning access to higher education in North Carolina.

The multiple critiques made by the undocumented students who weren't able to attend college and the alternative plans they made after high school were also forms of transformative resistance. I was a researcher from an American-centric perspective of higher education, that education is the best road toward economic stability and that higher education can open people's minds to new ideas, but the students forced me to recognize that my ideas toward higher education were rather narrow and limited. I had considered higher education as the only road to success; my students saw it as only one of the many roads to a better life. Many of the students who considered alternative plans after high school, because college was simply an unrealistic financial goal, denied the idea that college was everyone's dream.

Demonstrating his dual frame of reference (Suárez-Orozco, 1989), Saul, who was not able to gain admission to the highly selective university he had applied to, remarked that even though he wouldn't go to college right away, he did not view it as failure,

> Even if I don't go to college, I still think that I will have a better life than they [his parents] have had. I think that they have given me a better life here, than they would've been able to in Mexico. So if I don't go to college, I won't really mind because I think that's the way that it is, you know? For my dad's generation, the wish was for me to have a better life and I think I have, and for me, I think that I want to have my siblings have a better life.

The Mexican immigrant experience for many of the families that I worked with also mirrored the ideas of *bien educado* and *mal educado* that Guadalupe Valdes (1996) illustrated in her work. To be well educated is to be respectful and to take care of your family; to be poorly educated is to be disrespectful or to dishonor your family. Many of the teachers commented that although Latino parents had high educational aspirations for their children, working hard and developing a strong work ethic was the most valued ideal in the Mexican immigrant household. Several of the teachers also commented that Latino immigrant parents saw graduation from high school as an incredible accomplishment because it was a much higher level of educational attainment as compared to their own schooling experiences in Mexico:

Mr. John said,

> ....I don't see that and that's because the Latino guys are working, they work, and work is a big value in this community. This is the value that supersedes almost everything, working. I've talked to kids who can't come to an after school activity because they work because they have to pay off the couch in their living room. And I say wait a minute what are you talking about, and they are like yah, I've got bills to pay. And I asked them what kind of bills they have to pay, and they tell me that they have to pay for the sofa, and maybe the electricity for the month. I know a lot of kids who

contribute to the household. You can still go to school but you've got to work."

Ms. Stacey seconded Mr. John's remark:

They want things for their children that they were not able to have when they were younger. Initially I thought the Hispanic parents might be the same as the white parents but when I've talked to them during interviews most of them say that I want more for my child. They say things like, I want my children to have an easier life than I have had. Now I have had a few parents who feel like well they have had more education than me, so they don't need any more, like they would prefer that they drop out when they're 16 and to start working, but most of their parents feel like they want them to graduate high school.

Mr. Carlos also affirmed this view:

For most of the kids, they are going to be the first one in the family to graduate from high school, and that's an achievement in itself. Without seeing further beyond, without seeing college, graduating from high school is a big achievement in some of their families.

As students began to understand that they would not make it to college in their first year out of high school, they began to criticize the school system and society for not providing alternative opportunities for undocumented students after high school. They themselves made alternate plans, which did not include college. These decisions were based on providing support to their families and creating new learning opportunities for themselves beyond the traditional college pipeline. Saul, in particular, followed this path:

I'm a senior and I'm not really thinking about going to college anymore—got to work and pay bills. I probably like might go in a couple years but for right now I've decided what I need to do is work. My dad is struggling to pay the bills, payments like light bills, and I know now that if I got accepted I wouldn't really even be able to go because my dad needs my help....

I'm planning to leave and go with a friend who is currently working as a welder. He's even legal, and he is making over $21 per hour. And he's going to get me a job, he says that I'm at an advantage because I speak English so well. I think, you know that that's really a pretty good job. The job means that I will actually move around. He is currently in Asheville, but the job moves somewhere different every few months. The job means traveling all around the United States, which is the part that I like the most. And I have always dreamed about traveling around the United States...

I think that they [the school] could be encouraging other job opportunities. Like for example drafting, they have a class in drafting and it's actually a really very good class. And it teaches you how to read construction plans and everything. It's important to offer options for people that might not be going to college. They should be teaching people about the kind of job you can get if you don't go to college. They should be giving students different skills that they could use if they don't go to college...

While all of the students indicated that they would like to pursue higher education, if it was financially feasible, many believed that they could gain knowledge and have a rewarding life taking different paths that did not include a college experience. Tara Yosso's (Solórzano & Delgado-Bernal, 2001; Yosso, 2006) term, *resilient resistance,* is defined as, "surviving or succeeding through the educational pipeline," and does not take into account undocumented immigrant students' position. The gap in Yosso's theory, is that resilient resistance does not occur only within the confines of the educational pipeline. For the BGHS undocumented students, survival and success after high school took place both inside and outside the educational pipeline.

My analysis suggests that there is an additional vision of resilient resistance practiced by students who take an alternative trajectory from higher education and students who cannot legally access higher education. Because this resistance seems central to the values of the Mexican-immigrant undocumented experience, I call it *transnational*[20]

---

[20] This definition of transnational is meant to encompass Enrique Trueba's vision of the transnational student including a student who is immersed in their

resilient resistance (TRR). This type of resistance makes a critique of the system of the higher education system and takes active steps to find additional opportunities beyond the traditional education pipeline. This type of resistance is based on the values of the Mexican immigrant household and the policies which structure the undocumented student experience, and it offers agency for those students who seek to improve their lived conditions using alternative tactics when higher education may not be immediately accessible.

The values these undocumented students brought to BGHS were distinct from their American counterparts. These values included a communal view of social mobility. This communal view of social mobility is exemplified through how the students felt regarding whether or not their family could pay for them to attend community college as an out-of-state student. While most of the students did believe that their family could pull together enough money to pay for their community college tuition, each student reasoned that asking the family to sacrifice a large portion of their finances to go only toward their college tuition bill was selfish. This characteristic of communalism and self-sacrifice versus individualistic goals is a defining attribute of TRR.

When students made alternative plans for life after high school they also exhibited less rigidly defined definitions of success than their American counterparts. While these students all had the academic capability and motivation to continue to college, they also saw alternative experiences after high school as providing new opportunities to learn and grow. Students demonstrating TRR saw the opportunity to travel around the United States, the chance to provide for their family members and community, and the opportunity to become independent adults as stories of success just as laudable as obtaining a college degree.

TRR is central to the experiences of these undocumented students because not only does it critique narrow definitions of "success" in our society but it also highlights the costs that immigrant students must pay for mainstream success. All the students emphasized that the values of their Mexican households were often different than the message they received at school, and that academic success came with a certain level of forced accommodation. For example, participation in honors and AP courses caused isolation from their Latino peers. TRR also complicates

---

culture of origin (sometimes physically back and forth), as well as in their American lifestyle.

our ideas about both the costs and benefits of academic success through the more traditional education pipeline.

FIDEL'S JOURNEY TO UNIVERSITY: MULTIPLE OPPRESSIONS AND MULTIPLE RESISTANCE STRATEGIES

The students displayed differing sets of resisting behaviors. Sometimes those were self-defeating practices that re/created oppressive conditions; in other cases, students participated in transformative experiences which changed the course of their lives. As past research has emphasized, undocumented students live with intersecting oppressions including immigration status, race, class, and language; thus, many students do not select only one category of resistance behavior. Fidel, who is now a student at a four-year public university, helps us to understand the multiple and intersecting oppressions that occur for undocumented students and the varying ways in which they respond and resist. Fidel's resistance behaviors were tactics that he used cautiously as he moved through high school and into a four-year university, and these tactics continued as he began to navigate the higher education system. Getting access to higher education through admittance and scholarship was not the end of his struggle. His case study is a reflection of the multiple obstacles faced by undocumented students and the multiple resistance tactics that can be employed throughout the educational pipeline.

Fidel's struggle against the system began with his family's journey across the border of the United States. In Mexico his mother's occupation had been that of a street vendor, while his father drove a small delivery truck. When money no longer provided enough food to eat, and the family home was robbed, his father decided it was time to journey North. Fidel and his family crossed the border twice and twice were caught and sent back. Fidel recalled his mom's telling him to give a fake name when asked by *la migra* for information. Finally, on the third try he, his mother, and sister were able to cross the border in Arizona. This first act of resistance by his family was in response to the harsh conditions in Mexico and the opportunities that were available in the poultry factories in North Carolina.

As a child in the school system in North Carolina, Fidel excelled in his school work, learning English quickly and proving to his teachers that he could handle the transition into mainstream coursework. Fidel wanted to do well in school to please his family and his teachers; he did not remember that he and others were treated differently because of their Mexican immigrant background. Yet, as he recalled his schooling experiences, issues of racial inferiority framed the conversation:

> It was an English class and it was divided into two very distinct sides with Americans and "newcomers" and Mr. Garcia would teach us and then another teacher, Ms. Salsbury, would teach the American kids. And then it got to the point that I was too smart for the Hispanic side and they moved me. And it was so hard. I cried that day; I couldn't take it. It was hard to move to the other side.

Fidel also described ESL classes through a deficit perspective and hinted at distinctions between the regular classes for American kids: "Well, basically yah, well in sixth grade I no longer had all ESL classes it was only a period, I had no more math, social studies, English, this time I had all normal classes except ESL. And then in the seventh grade I had *normal* everything, no more ESL."

As Fidel continued through elementary school and entered high school, his residency status remained a secret. Fidel described his doing well in school as centered in a conformist resistance framework. As he began the college application process, he decided to use the system that existed to negotiate his college application process, while at the same time recognizing that, in fact, it was highly unlikely that he would be able to go to college because of his undocumented status. When I asked him why he continued to do so well in school, despite his undocumented status he replied,

> Well I don't know, well you know I do know why I take AP classes. It is because when I found out I was not going to be able to go to college I sort of got very depressed. Well, then I found out that these courses could give me college credit then I thought, well maybe that is the closest I am going to get to college. I mean a real college class, and that's why I work so hard. Last year I was under the notion that I was never going to go to college so I thought that this is the closest I am ever going to get so I'll just do it.

As the year went on Fidel began to negotiate the college application process by utilizing various tactics. Throughout the process he only approached and told trusted teachers and confidants about his undocumented status. He then systematically made choices about the college application process: He applied for fee waivers for all of the colleges he applied to, and he narrowed his decision to one "dream" college and others that would be the cheapest schools for out-of-state students. Throughout the process, he asked for help only on specific issues. Fidel strategically approached teacher allies for help with essay writing, college information, and advice on scholarships and financial aid. When I ask Fidel who he approached for help, the following exchange occurred:

> Janet: Is there anyone specific who helped or encouraged you to think about college?
>
> Fidel: Well not really, there are a lot of people that have helped me because I've been asking them. I mean, I haven't been saying that I didn't know anything, I've been asking for specific help and they have sort of offered. Ms. Olivia at the high school has been really helpful, and that's about it. She is the one who helped me do the entire University X application and all the essays. It was really a lot of work.

In the spring of his junior year, teacher allies Ms. Olivia, Ms. Stacey and Mr. Mark approached the Latino Outreach program and told me that they worked with an outstanding senior who would likely be unable to go to college because of his documentation status. Once I was made aware of Fidel's situation, I began working with him. Fidel made other contacts with a liaison at the Latino Outreach program, and a senior professor at a university, who encouraged him to work hard so that a university might be able to produce scholarship dollars for him. Recognizing an important ally, Fidel responded to all requests that the professor made of him by participating in an early college experience at the high school, taking as many AP courses as possible in his senior year, and meeting with the professor whenever he came to visit the high school. Fidel's relationship with me grew as well during this process. His year in the research study he sent his essays to me for editing and improvement, attended every Latino Outreach event even though he was not officially a member of the program, and researched and applied to alternative private universities that I encouraged him to consider. Fidel's comments revealed the strategic nature of these relationships:

> I applied to University X and that's it. I have applications for other places and I'm still waiting first to hear from them. Since University X might be the only place that will accept me with Dr. R's help, and other schools also charge out of state tuition, University X might be the only one willing to help me with that. I'm applying to other places that have cheap out-of-state tuition and private schools since they don't have to follow guidelines of public schools.

> He says he (Dr. R.) can help me with money problems. "You can apply and you have to get in on your own," but he can try to help with money issues. He said, "I can help with money issues."

His use of his teachers, of the resources of the Latino Outreach program, and the university professor were well thought out, which showed that Fidel understood they would help negotiate his admission to a four-year university.

Throughout the college application process Fidel faced more obstacles, and it was by contending with these obstacles that he moved from conformist resistance (trying to operate within the system with little criticism of it) to more transformative and resilient resistance. When he had trouble filling out international applications, finding scholarships that he would be eligible for as an undocumented student, and conducting college application interviews where he feared revealing his status could place his family in jeopardy, Fidel expressed his anger at the entire situation. In our first interview together in the fall of his senior year he expressed outrage at a tutoring program in which he participated in to assist ESL learners with math. While other students, who were citizens, were paid for tutoring younger students, Fidel had to volunteer his time. He mentioned, "Yah, well the funny thing was, two years ago, I did it, and they paid me, and it wasn't a problem. I was paid, and I was the ESL everything tutor, and that was my sophomore year. I guess I was breaking other rules because I wasn't 15 and I didn't fill out the whole application, but they wanted me so they just paid me. And now, all of sudden, they won't break this rule and I don't really understand." Even though Fidel was angry he continued to tutor students because he remembered what it was like to be in their shoes and wanted to help as many "newcomer students" as possible.

As Fidel became angrier with his situation and with the laws regarding undocumented high school students in the state of North Carolina, he began to channel this energy into the creative outlet of writing. When he first wrote about his experiences, he considered putting out his story publicly in the school newspaper but then reconsidered:

> I actually wrote an essay about that [writing about being brought to the United States and how it was not his fault] and I wanted to put it in the newspaper. It was like an essay where I pretended I was the mastermind behind the whole thing [my parents coming here] and me getting into the US, and at the very end it is revealed that I was only nine years old. And the main message of this essay was that you can not judge a person, not a child that was only nine years old.

Although Fidel ultimately decided that sharing his story in the public forum of the school newspaper would not be a smart move, for he would completely reveal himself to the school (a safety tactic he employed), the essay for his college applications was a highly political form of external resistance which made a very compelling critique of the system. This college essay displayed a very distinct transformation in Fidel's understanding and response to the current structures in the state. One teacher expressed pride about the college essay he wrote saying, "The writing was good, and it was in his voice, and it really expressed who he was." The college essay appears below:

> I believe that certain people are given talents, not because they want to because fate had it that they would have them. When I knew that I didn't have one, I made it my mission to learn one. Three years ago I gave myself the mission, of what I then considered the ludicrous and insane idea, of writing a book. Today, I stand with two folders filled with more than one thousand pages. I gave myself that assignment to see I if could commit myself to something as big as writing a book, and I didn't fail. The book I chose to write was in the genre of fantasy. I have toiled with the ideas in my head for three years, but all has been training for the one thing that matters to me the most. Three years ago, I didn't want to write a fantasy book, I wanted to write the story of what many go through to come here. The story of crossing the border. I wanted to

write story of why two Mexican parents would risk their lives and those of their son's and daughter's to come to this country. The story of what many people who consider themselves Hispanic don't see. The story of the situations of my home country of Mexico, from my city of Tuxtepec to the border. I want to tell the story of the boy who had to steal his school materials, the one who had to walk past the garbage dump and see others kids like himself looking for anything to eat, the one who had to deliver *Biocult* on countless afternoons and weekends up until 10:00 p.m.. That story is worth telling, even if it is mine. The writing of the fantasy book has been a test to prepare to write about what really matters to me: my people. Three years ago, I decided not to dishonor them by writing anything about them because I was young and immature. Today, I feel the same way but that is because it is an honor for me to start in this endeavor. I feel the time is right, the country has taken to the worst on its xenophobic agenda. It is time to tell the story of that little boy, to show that we are not criminals but innocents.

The feelings of anger towards people who blame the children who are caught in the middle, of wanting to create understanding of why people cross the border, and of understanding for his people and what they have to offer the United States are all beautifully expressed in the college admission essay created by Fidel. This essay represented a "coming out" in his writing. As Solórzano and Delgado-Bernal (2001) point out, "Although the act of political writing can be a form of internal transformational resistance, once it is published or made public, it can be a very powerful form of external transformational resistance."(326) By taking this step, Fidel crossed from internal to external resistance and publicly stood up for himself and his community. This was a transformative point in his journey.

Fidel's essays and his ultimate admission to a selective four-year university that also provided four years of private scholarship funding for him revealed that, although the structures create many difficult barriers for undocumented students, the agency practiced by students and the utilization of tactics to negotiate the terrain can ultimately create moments of resilient resistance (Solórzano & Delgado-Bernal, 2001; Yosso, 2006) inside the educational pipeline. The resourcefulness, the social capital, and the tenacity of this one student created just one opportunity in the state of North Carolina. While

Fidel's story is a victory to be celebrated, the other students were unable to leverage themselves into college after high school.

After Fidel accessed the college pipeline, the tactics he practiced in high school continue to be utilized in his journey through college. When Fidel began the college school year, he continued to face numerous obstacles that other first-year students attending college did not: being approached by a major news magazine to tell his story, and making the choice not to come forward publicly to protect both himself and the university he is now attending, trying to figure out whether or not it was safe to tell his roommate and new friends about his personal situation, and trying to cope with parents who had shared his story with members of his church and wondering whether or not he would be "found out."

In addition, Fidel had to consider whether or not to register for selective service, how was he going to get a North Carolina bank account in order to cash his scholarship checks, or how to register for SEVIS as an international student who wasn't really international. He wondered how to approach his professors regarding the fact that English was not his first language and that he would need extra help on his writing because of it. He also pondered how to handle himself in the first-year seminar that discussed immigration issues and the current immigration debate. All of these issues continue to create obstacles and negotiations that his American classmates need not consider in their first year of college. Yet, through all of this, Fidel continues to persevere, practicing tactics of resistance in both internal and external forms. While he is only one student, his presence in the system represents the possibilities for personal and societal transformation. He is now in the higher education system, and because of his experiences, may likely be a student who changes the terrain for those that follow.

CHAPTER 8

Counternarratives to the Label of "Illegal"

Past research on Latinos and education provides an understanding that historically inadequate educational conditions have limited equal access and opportunities for Latinos in U.S. schooling (Donato, 1997; Garcia, 2001, Gonzalez, 1990; San Miguel, 1987). Recognition of this history has been a starting point for Latino Critical (LatCrit) theorists. In addition to this history, LatCrit built on the foundation of critical race theory's (CRT) use of voice and narrative, and expanded the use of counterstorytelling. For CRT and LatCrit theorists, "Counterstorytelling is a way of telling the story of those experiences that are often not told and a tool for analyzing and challenging stories of those in power and whose story is a natural party of the dominant discourse." (Solórzano & Yosso, 2001, p. 475). Samuel Huntington (2004) expresses a particularly vicious, but sadly typical, version of the dominant discourse:

> The persistent inflow of Hispanic immigrants threatens to divide the United States into two peoples, two cultures, and two languages. Unlike past immigrant groups, Mexicans and other Latinos have not assimilated into mainstream U.S. culture, forming instead their own political and linguistic enclaves — from Los Angeles to Miami—and rejecting the Anglo-Protestant values that built the American dream. The United States ignores this challenge at its peril... Sosa ends his book, *The Americano Dream*, with encouragement for aspiring Hispanic entrepreneurs. "The Americano dream?" he asks. "It exists, it is realistic, and it is there for all of us to share." Sosa is wrong. There is no Americano dream. There is only the American dream created by an Anglo-Protestant society. Mexican-Americans will share in that dream and in that society only if they dream in English. (Huntington, 2004, p.13)

In an earlier work Richard Delgado (1989) opposed such inflexible mainstream definitions with a more generous explanation of why we should value counterstories:

> Reality is fixed not a given, we construct it through our conversations, through our lives together. Racial and class-based isolation prevents the hearing of diverse stories and counterstories. It diminishes the conversations through which we create reality, and construct our communal lives. Deliberately exposing oneself to counterstories can avoid that impoverishment, heighten "suspicion" and can enable the listener and the teller to build a world richer than either could make alone. On another occasion, the listener will be the teller, sharing a secret, a piece of information, or an angle of vision that will enrich the former teller, and so on dialectically, enrich the tapestry of conversation in stories. (Delgado, 1989, p.2439)

Latino Critical Race theorists Daniel Solórzano and Tara Yosso (2001) posited that counterstories serve four theoretical, methodological, and pedagogical functions:

They can build community among those at the margins of society by putting a human and familiar face to educational theory and practice.

They challenge perceived wisdom of those at society's center by providing a context to understand and transform established belief systems.

They can open new windows into the reality of those at the margins of society by showing the possibilities beyond the ones they live and demonstrating that they are not alone in that position.

They can teach others that by combining elements from both the story and the current reality, one can construct another world that is richer than either the story or the reality alone. (pg. 475)

The *counterstory* offers an alternative to the mainstream educational and legal discourse. The *counterstories* provided by CRT and LatCrit theorists challenge *majoritarian stories* that exist and are created by the dominant discourse (Solórzano & Yosso, 2001).

Majoritarian stories, for their part, generate from the history of racial privilege in the United States. Their hegemonic power lies in how these stories appear natural and how they become widely accepted. These stories, when examined more critically, display layers of assumptions and myths that have been created not by people in the positions of subordination but in positions of domination.[21]

With counternarratives, CRT and LatCrit theorists disrupt the majoritarian stories that have been woven into the dominant discourse. Examining the majoritarian beliefs that people hold about citizenship status, as well as the beliefs that are held about undocumented students'

---

[21] For example, Emilio Parrado (Parrado & Valencia, 2010) conducted research that interrogates past health statistics, which reported extremely high pregnancy rates of young Latina/o mothers in North Carolina. He has found that the statistics were incorrect, yet for years no one questioned the validity of the numbers. Parrado claims that researchers did not examine these unusually high numbers, when published several years ago, because of generally accepted beliefs that young and multiple pregnancies are a cultural trait of young Latinas.

educational capabilities, helps us to understand how these beliefs are used to subordinate and marginalize them inside and outside school.

MAJORITARIAN STORIES ABOUT UNDOCUMENTED STUDENTS IN NORTH CAROLINA

In *Education in the New Latino South*, Enrique Murillo (2002) painted a complex picture of how the Anglo majority in Sunder Crossings, North Carolina, constructed the influx of Latino newcomers to the town as a problem and then called those newcomers themselves "problems." To Murillo, this "label of other" was a way for the dominant (white) community to discipline the immigrants who arrived in Sunder Crossings. Murillo builds his case through evidence of poor treatment of Latino newcomers by the government, the education system and the general public reception. He emphasized that the power structures in Sunder Crossings descended not only from the historic colonialism of the United States, but also from the particularly oppressive racist nature of the South.

Murillo (2002) cited newspaper reports, radio shows and public service flyers to illustrate myths that Mexicans were "takers" and not "givers." He commented, "Latinos were often thought of and portrayed as problematic, chaotic, dirty, and unintelligent." (p.230) Murillo emphasized that people in the town do not want their resources threatened or jeopardized by a new population of people they see as "illegal" and "undeserving" of those public resources.

Fear regarding scarce resources was especially evident in North Carolinians' argument against giving in-state tuition to undocumented students. When House Bill 1183 (the state version of the DREAM Act) was introduced in the fall of 2005 in North Carolina many local residents believed that undocumented students would be taking admission spots of North Carolina citizens. In the *Raleigh News and Observer* people articulated these beliefs by saying, "If you commence to letting these illegals in front of your natural citizens, don't tell me that you're not cutting space out for them. I just can't see doing that. You know if it's going to cut out more of our children and grandchildren then I'm personally against it. They are taking seats away from students that are here legally." (Stancill, 2005)

Behind the common belief about scarcity of resources was anger that illegal immigrants were being rewarded for breaking the law. The notion of illegality was tied to what a student deserved to receive. During the fall of 2006, immigration lawyer and higher education scholar Michael A. Olivas came to the University of North Carolina's

(UNC) campus to speak on the DREAM Act. Following his lecture, an article summarizing it appeared in the *Daily Tar Heel* newspaper. Later in the week, online responses to this article displayed the beliefs of different members of the UNC campus community in responses to quotations that the article put in from Olivas' talk:

> *"These are very worthy students that otherwise would have no options at all.?*
> --No other options???? I suppose not breaking the law isn't an option?

> *"Qualified candidates would receive six years of temporary citizenship and would be granted full citizenship upon completion of two years of college or military service."*
> --Wow, what a horrible idea. Why don't we throw our entire immigration system out the window and physically erase our national borders. I mean, that's gotta be the next logical step, right? If illegal aliens can earn citizenship simply by sitting in a classroom and sleeping for 2 years, why don't we allow people who live in the country formerly known as Mexico to sleep through class and be citizens of the country formerly known as America?

> *"[S]tudents who have been here all their lives..."*
> --Well, they can't have been here all their lives, or they'd be citizens. That's that pesky country-of-birth clause.

> *"They are not able to have a post-secondary education simply because of their status."*
> --Umm... Yeah. That's kinda the point isn't it? Have you READ the Constitution lately? It begins, "We the people OF THE UNITED STATES..." If you aren't a citizen, you DON'T get to enjoy the rights and privileges of the citizens.[22]

---

[22] These were online comments in response to an article written in the Daily Tar Heel by Stacy Wells entitled, "College Dreams Hang in the Balance." This was retrieved on November 20, 2007 at http://media.www.dailytarheel. commedia/storage/paper885/news/2006/11/16/University/College.Dreams.Han g.In.Balance2463311.shtml?sourcedomain=www.dailytarheel.com&MIIHost= media.collegepublisher.com

Later in the week, an article in the UNC school magazine the *Blue & White* explored what it might be like to live on campus as an undocumented student. This article also contained comments from UNC alumni who believed that undocumented students should have access to neither K-12 education nor higher education (Younger, 2006).

> These people are now talking about rights, committed a felony when they entered the country illegally. As felons, please tell me about what rights they have other than trial and rapid expulsion—Thomas H. Campbell Jr., UNC Chapel Hill Alumnus

> Even these freebies are not enough for illegal immigrants, especially Hispanics. They want schools to hire teachers to teach them English; free college educations (for which most citizens pay 30-35K per year); free health care; free milk for their (many) children, then they send money back to their country of origin to bring more illegals here for the U.S. to support. Then they have the unmitigated gall to protest for better treatment—Patricia C. Harris, UNC Chapel Hill Alumnus

Numerous other articles in both local and national newspapers have reflected similar ideas; rewarding undocumented students with taxpayer subsidized education is not an entitlement illegal immigrants deserved.

The undeservingness of access to higher education for undocumented students also was tied to the belief that undocumented students did not have the ability to succeed in higher education. This argument was tied intimately to their status as Mexican illegals. In one article in the National Review Online, Peter Kirsanow (2006) contends that if undocumented students were to be allowed in-state tuition status they would be unnecessarily rewarded twice, once for being illegal and again as a member of a minority group that would receive affirmative action benefits. Kirsanow argued:

> Illegal Immigrants who are members of preferred minority groups are entitled to other benefits unavailable to the vast majority of American citizens. At some schools

> applicants are up to 100 times more likely to be admitted than similarly situated non-preferred comparatives. Affirmative Action programs are structured at some schools in a way that, beyond a minimum level of qualification preferred, minority applicants are virtually guaranteed admission.
>
> Many high school seniors will soon discover that having a 4.0 GPA, 1500 SATS and dazzling extracurricular activities means less than having the proper ethnicity. And being a U.S. citizen means nothing at all.

The argument that somehow minority students would receive a privilege because of their ethnicity and not their ability, and that they lacked academic ability, was an undercurrent in numerous conversations I had during the data collection process for this research.

When making individual phone calls to admission offices regarding their undocumented student policies, I was told by one small, private liberal arts college in North Carolina that it had a general policy not to work with undocumented students, but that this was rarely an issue since they had a fairly selective admission standards and did not have a large number of "those students" applying to their university. A county school board official told me that I would not find students to participate in my research at Benson Guthrie High School because although they did have undocumented students attending BGHS, none of these undocumented students who were "college capable." Teacher allies also remarked that there were particular teachers at the school who equated immigrant students' lack of English with lack of academic ability. Oliverez' research (Oliverez, 2005a; Oliverez, 2005b) in California also has demonstrated teachers' deficit beliefs that undocumented students are not seen as college material. Although it took different shapes and forms, this majoritarian story regarding the lack of academic capability of undocumented Mexican immigrants was clearly present.

In addition there was general sentiment that undocumented students and their families had chosen to come to the United States on their own free will and, thus, ultimately deserved no pity because now they refused to assimilate properly into the American (Anglo) culture. These types of ideas spiral into other general stories that people have created about immigrants including that they are 1) unwilling to learn

English and 2) unsupportive of their children in the education system. Finally, since one of the important tools counterstory has is to open new windows into the reality of those at the margins of society, it is important to illustrate that many of the U.S. students at BGHS who attended class, played on the same sports teams and interacted in the halls each day with their classmates were completely unaware that their undocumented peers lived in differing realities. Their inability to recognize this situation was reflected in numerous observations and in interviews with their teachers including these below:

> Ms. Olivia: One of them last year, you know, Mark Smith (a pseudonym) the valedictorian, well I finally had to explain to Mark the situation about the student behind him, Stella Garcia (a pseudonym), she can't go to college, do you understand this? She's not going to get any financial aid even though she's going to be able to get in. I said, this is why this is a messed up way to do business. And he was like, you're kidding? And I was like, no.

> Mr. David: My upper-middle-class white students, they are not in the same reality. When I talked to my cross-country runners about immigration, it doesn't even register. You realize that you are in classes with students who can't go to college because they are undocumented, the way it stands right now they won't be able to go to college. It doesn't even cross their mind. You think that the only place they see each other is at school, and in the school I think there is a certain sense of a level playing field. But then when I drive my Latino students home to their trailer parks and my middle-class student home to his three-bedroom house, you really see that their realities are totally different. And it's not that one group is trying to be malicious and trying to say, "I'm trying to keep them down," it's just that they don't even see the parallel realities.

> Ms. Stacey: Fidel's friends in the AP program are aware (about his personal situation). But kind of globally, like most adolescents they are only concerned with themselves. They might be kind of tangentially aware of it but because it's not their problem, they are not terribly worried about it.

Counterstories' powers lie in their ability to present a different reality than what has come to be "accepted truth."   The following counterstories challenge and disrupt the majoritarian stories which distort the reality and the value of the undocumented high school student. These stories can teach others, including peers, teachers, law and policymakers that majoritarian stories are causing us to miss out on the value undocumented students would add in both the higher education community and to our ever-changing global society as a whole.

THE RIGHT STUFF

In the spring of 2006, I had been working with most of the students in some capacity at their school for between nine months to a year. While four of the five seniors waited to hear whether they had been admitted to University X, I sat down to pen a letter to one of University X's admission officers:

> I just received an e-mail this evening from one of my juniors in the Latino Outreach Program informing me that he is quitting the program because he knows that he will never be able to afford college in the United States because of his legal status. Receiving this e-mail has been heartbreaking but it has prompted me to send one last e-mail to the admission office regarding students at BGHS.

> While I know that you will not admit all the students, I do want you to know that I personally believe that any of the students I have been working with including Fidel, Frances, Carmen, and Saul all deserve the chance to succeed and to reach their academic potential. While none of them may be the "perfect candidate" each of them has wonderful characteristics and has displayed a resilience I have seen in few students that I have worked with over the years. Whether it is Fidel's brilliant mind, Saul's leadership capabilities or Frances and Carmen's tenacity and spirit, I felt compelled to at least write to you one more time to urge you to take a long, hard look at each of these candidates. I know realistically that you won't accept them all but, if none is accepted I will be shocked and disheartened that a university that claims it is for the "people of North Carolina" is essentially turning its back on such an important community of students.

> I know that you are a great advocate for Latino students and I
> know that this e-mail may make no difference, but I felt
> compelled this evening to send you a message regarding
> students I think are deserving and wonderful candidates for
> admission.

Throughout my own academic career I had focused on high-achieving
Latina/o students and at this basic level, these undocumented students
were no different.   But, as I learned more about their individual
situations, I realized that these brilliant, talented and academically
qualified high school seniors would be unable to attend college without
a great deal of financial support. If there were five of them as talented
as these individuals in a senior class of 150 students, I began to imagine
just how many more must exist throughout high schools in the state.
Throughout my data collection, the majoritarian stories constructed
about lack of academic capability of undocumented students were
consistently negated with counterstories displaying the talents and
academic capabilities of the undocumented students.   These stories
were shared by their teachers, witnessed by me as the director of the
Latino Outreach program and demonstrated by the actions of these five
undocumented students. Themes surrounding the students' abilities
included themes of academic capabilities, resourcefulness and hard
work.

ACADEMIC CAPABILITY

When I was first informed by the county administrator that I would not
find undocumented students who were capable of college level work, I
knew this to be an inaccurate portrayal of the undocumented students at
Benson Guthrie High School. Once I came to know these students,
received copies of their high school transcripts, and spoke with their
high school teachers, I felt pity for the administrator who knew so little
about the students in his own county.

Figure 2: Students Academic Backgrounds

Name	Age of Arrival in U.S.	Class Rank	# of Honors (AP) Classes	ACT Score	H.S. Education Track	Post-H.S.
Fidel	11	18/136 (13%)	15(7)	26	College Prep	College/ 4-year
Ricardo	7	15/136 (11%)	14(2)	20	College Prep	Oddjobs
Carmen	11	46/136 (33%)	8(2)	21	Career Prep	Working fast food
Saul	11	39/136 (28%)	11(2)	17	College Prep	Working as welder
Frances	15/ varied	36/136 (26%)	7(0)	18	Career Prep	Returned to Mexico

I pitied the administrator for his mindset that because these students had started in ESL classes somehow made them forever incapable of college level work. These students took honors level coursework, and had done so for quite some time. In my initial interviews about their school backgrounds, many of the students talked about how ESL coursework no longer was necessary for them at the high school level. Regardless of what courses they took, ESL classes do not signal incapability. In addition to being transitioned out of ESL courses, many of them had been singled out as top performers in their classes:

> They would put immigrant students in freshmen courses, no matter how much English they seemed to know. I mean ESL is not bad, for students who need to learn English, but I didn't need to learn English. In the beginning I was in ESL classes and I didn't need them.
>
> *--Frances, who arrived as a junior from Mexico and who took multiple honors courses during her junior and senior years.*

> I got out of ESL classes in the eighth grade. Since then, I only have had regular classes, and in the eighth grade I came out

with high ranking in all my classes. I was the student of the year and everything. That's what gets me the most. Most people know me because I was such a good student.

--Saul who took AP Spanish, Honors English, and Calculus as a senior.

Janet: So, you came and you told me that you were really, really smart in Mexico and you are obviously very smart here because your teachers brag on you quite a bit.

Fidel: Well, that's what they say, but I don't know (laughs shyly).

--Fidel, who took AP English, AP Calculus, AP Environmental Science, and AP Government during his senior year.

In addition to these students, Fidel noted that there were other undocumented students at BGHS who also shared in their academic ability: "Why me, why Frances, why Carmen—why are we some of the only students picked for your research? There are other young students who are real smart, maybe I mean not exactly like me and taking four AP classes, but they are still real smart."

ACADEMIC CAPABILITY VIEWED THROUGH TEACHERS' PERSPECTIVES

Along with the high school transcripts, which spoke for themselves, the ability and potential of these undocumented students was a focal point of the majority of the interviews that were conducted with the teachers at Benson Guthrie High School. While the teacher allies recognized that other teachers at BGHS had deficit perspectives of Latino kids who can't speak English well, the teacher allies thought most undocumented students proved those ideas dead wrong. Stacey admitted the following regarding some of her colleagues:

I think that there are some teachers here at BGHS, who don't believe that Hispanic students can succeed just because they can't speak English well. Sometimes when a teacher sees that Hispanic student's last name, they decide that they can't speak English and that they are not very smart. And I'm like wait a minute here, you got that wrong.

> I think it varies, I think that if a teacher knows that they were born here, they might think that they are better student. The ones that some teachers aren't sure about are the ones who haven't been here for very long and don't speak very good English. And then there are students like Elario (pseudonym of a recent immigrant student) who come in and pick up the language so fast that I think they make teachers think twice about those types of attitudes. Like in the math department, Elario is in Algebra I and he's got a 99, so I'm trying to move him into an advanced math class next year. But I know I'm going to have to fight one of the teachers in that department, a teacher that I think has low expectations for Hispanic students. I'm trying to get a release from his End of Course Tests (EOC), because his transcripts from his country of origin say that he already has had a lot of the math classes and he doesn't need to take them again. That's why he sitting in Algebra I bored. The math department is going to fight me on it because they will say that they will have to be able to speak English, and I think that numbers are numbers.

Linked with the general deficit beliefs some teachers held about Latino students, Ms. Stacey clearly identified that time in the country (and, thus, in many cases spoken English skills) and citizenship status (whether they are born here or not) framed how teachers felt about a student's academic capability. Despite the fact that this particular student could provide transcripts showing his ability in math, the department fought to keep him out of advanced coursework. While Ms. Stacey saw that some departments made more focused efforts to work with new immigrant students, she still thought teachers often held deficit perspectives of Mexican-origin students:

> The departments are really different, like the science department. They just tried to jump right in and do the best they can with students who have limited English. I've never had a teacher in the science department say the types of things that the teachers do in the math department. The science department is great, they try to get tutors, and they try to get all the help they can for those students. The math department is really difficult, because they would rather see students in math type 1 so they don't have to have the classes like Algebra

II and Geometry overloaded. They also feel like, if only the best and brightest are in Algebra II, then their End of Course test scores will be higher. As a whole, they seem frustrated when I put a low C student in one of their classes. They accuse me of not giving the student a chance and I feel like it's the other way around. They are not giving the student a chance.

I know a teacher, who says, "How am I to teach history or U.S. history to Mexican students? They don't care about our history. They would rather have a sheltered ESL class about history.

Not only are deficit perspectives about Latino students illustrated in the comments, but also a nativist perspective about whom knowledge and learning belongs in the U.S. public school system. While Ms. Stacey found that these teachers' arguments defied the facts, other teachers, like Mr. David, felt that anyone who had such deficit perspectives about undocumented students simply was unintelligent. When I asked Mr. David about the views of the school district administrator, who felt that there were not college-capable undocumented students at BGHS, he simply replied,

Well, you need to understand you're dealing with the dumb ass. I think his comments are a perfect example of sheer stupidity. And there's just no way around it, well that's not even a feasible notion. I just don't even know how to respond you on that. There are just stupid people everywhere as much as you'd like to think that there aren't.

Teacher allies also fought against the belief held by the general public that such students would be unfairly "rewarded" for being illegal by using their academic capabilities to earn a spot at college and universities around the state. Fidel, the most academically accomplished student within the group, often was promoted as a deserving student. Ms. Olivia commented, "Fidel's academic progress, his volunteer efforts: He has earned his spot. You have to make the argument that people have earned their place." Mr. David also argued on Fidel's behalf, saying, "Fidel's nature is, he's just a dork. His very desire is to learn more and to want to read more. He is a natural student." Ms. Jennifer also emphasized the academic ability of the young women: "Carmen and Frances, I can see their motivation because they are genuinely bright, and can certainly go to college." Many of the teacher allies stressed that because these undocumented students were bright, teachers enjoyed working with them and encouraging them in school:

> Then you have teachers that know these kids have real talent. I mean to meet Fidel, he is a real intellectual, and Ms. Olivia recognized that, and she worked with him. So you've got teachers that will work with kids. –Ms. Jennifer

The teacher allies worked hard with the undocumented students on their college essays, with their AP homework, as they prepared to take AP tests, and while they studied for their ACT and SAT tests. They were well aware that all of these students were in honors and AP coursework and held top spots in their senior class. The teachers believed these students, whom they had helped prepare to attend and complete college coursework, were ready to do so, but clearly the policies in place would deter their achievement. They wanted to see these children become lawyers, doctors, teachers and architects not only because of personal attachments to these students, but also because their assessment of these students' academic abilities to reach such goals.

Ultimately, teachers agreed that academic ability was no barrier for these students; the major barrier that existed was the lack of access to higher education. Stacey summed it up well:

> So we don't care what race they are or what their background is, but we want all of them to push themselves to do the honors and AP if they are capable. So now my Hispanic students that have done that well, now they're ready and they want to go to college and that's where the barrier is. And you know they're ready to go to college and ready to do the work.

RESOURCEFULNESS AND RESILIENCY

Many of these students, much like other undocumented students across the United States, have lived with poverty, hunger, separation from family, and adjustment to a completely new environments. These students coped with grace and a resiliency that has been highlighted in other research on other students in their situation (DeLeon, 2005, Perez et al. 2009). Still, the strength it must take for a student to endure such struggle and to continue to flourish in a new environment Mr. John, emphasized to me,

> Every kid that you have met at that school has come across that desert, in some way they have crossed that desert, sometimes the cross is easy, sometimes it's very difficult, sometimes people barely managed to survive, so they have been through the fire in other ways that [other] kids haven't. And they take it all in stride. It's a wonderful quality.

The resiliency and resourcefulness of these students are a necessary skill that must be developed in order to live the second-class level of citizenship that too often comes with immigration to the United States. Some, but not all, of the teachers felt hopeful that despite the financial barriers for college, the students eventually would find a way to obtain a college degree. Mr. John commented, "The kids will find a way to get things. They are extremely resourceful. So that's why the college thing, sometimes I get down about it and other times I don't. The population is very resourceful and they have overcome things, all kinds of things."

One teacher ally suggested that because of the resourcefulness of the undocumented students, denying them from access to the resource of higher education would be a decision that the state would later regret. The teacher talked about the difficulty between living as undocumented when they were in high school and living as "illegal" when they went to work. The teacher warned of the social dangers that exist by keeping an educated population from accessing higher education resources:

> These kids are protected at this time in high school. They use their real names, and they live in a bubble, where they live legally. But after they graduate, they are entering into an illegal world, where they will become workers, so being a supervisor might be as high as these kids will go until their papers are checked, and these kids can be fired at any moment. One of my students is working in construction. They have to enter into this secret underground world now, but they're smart, and they're educated, and they will become fed up with what they have.

This teacher's comments regarding the resourcefulness of undocumented students also warns about the possibilities that could occur when enough educated undocumented students become fed up with the current policies and laws that exist in the state. The teacher suggested that not recognizing the abilities and resourcefulness of these students may have more severe consequences once a critical mass exists. The seeds for acts of resistance and the development of contentious practices (Holland & Lave, 2000) are sown each day the state continues to deny students access to higher education.

WORK ETHIC

As Carmen and I sat in the café and visit, I realized that our time was coming to an end. She had rushed over to the café after school, but informed me on the phone that she would need to leave at a quarter to five to get to her job at the fast-food restaurant. When she left, she gave me a warm hug and a gentle smile. Many who know her well often comment that she never seems to wear a frown. I think about her school schedule, which includes honors classes, traveling three afternoons a week to the local community college for dual enrollment credits, soccer practice including games on the weekends and on top of all of that, her job. Her earnings at the fast-food restaurant contribute to her aunt and uncle's household, where she lives. During the school week, her "part-time" job includes Tuesdays 5-9 p.m., Friday evenings from 5-11 p.m. and on weekends working early mornings.

The beliefs held by the general public that undocumented immigrants have come to the United States for the "freebies" of public education and public services certainly do not reflect the social reality for the hard-working Mexican families and children in Sunder Crossings. Four of the five students held at least part-time jobs before they had graduated from high school. Saul worked upwards of 45 hours per week at a popular fast-food restaurant, and he had been invited by the company to train as a manager. He and several other of the Latino immigrants at this restaurant had been invited to take management training because of their commitment to their work and their leadership in the working environment.

All of the students who worked did so to help their family. The expectation for them to contribute to their families was unquestioned as part of their duties to their family households. While the students also kept a portion of their paycheck for themselves (some had saved enough to purchase a used car), a significant portion went to help pay for utility bills or rent in the households where they lived.

They also balanced the work ethic toward those jobs with hard work at school. While they maintained high grades in their honors coursework, several students served as after-school tutors for ESL students, and two of the five students participated in state-championship sports teams. These students also were active in the Hispanic student club on campus, and Carmen served as the president of this organization. To say that these students were "takers" and not "givers" within their school was not a justifiable claim for anyone to make.

Teacher allies perceived the hard work ethic that these students displayed as an ideal that was upheld at home and transferred to the academic environment once they got to school. Ms. Jennifer, thought that this was particularly relevant to the Latina girls: "In the home they have to be so responsible and organized, and so brilliant [that] it's carried on in the academic environment of school!" Teacher allies who worked with recent immigrant students felt especially positive about what hard workers these students were in their classrooms. "My newcomers (students) work like dogs, and they are so keen to please! And I think that's part of the reason I enjoy teaching them, they are so keen to please you as a teacher," explained Ms. Stacey.

One teacher ally thought the hard work ethic was closely linked to the undocumented student experience. As a seasoned veteran of the school Mr. Carlos had seen the attitudes of the students change once they became legal permanent residents and U.S. citizens. When I asked him whether or not he saw differences between the undocumented Latino students and their legal permanent resident and U.S. citizen counterparts he answered,

> The undocumented students: they know that they don't have a say. In terms of how they see the future, documented students don't care too much. The future will come eventually, and it won't be bad; undocumented students don't know if they're going to be here tomorrow, so they live in the present, not the future. I'm sorry, I mean to say that documented kids take things for granted. On the other hand, the undocumented students know they have to fight for everything.

This fighting attitude was assessed by Mr. Carlos as a positive attribute that pushed undocumented students to work harder and excel in the classroom.

THE COUNTERSTORY OF MIGRATION TO NORTH CAROLINA

> I think in a lot of ways the corporations, our American corporations want undocumented workers because it is the perfect system. And it's a bad system; there are a lot of victims of this system, lots and lots of victims. Just look at our students. They are the victims in that, when there were six or seven years old, nobody said to them, do you want to go to the United States. It was pushed on them, it wasn't an option for them. –Mr. David

It was a Thursday evening and as the co-instructor in a qualitative research methods class, I was sharing the experiences of linking theory to data. When I explained why I chose to use critical race theory, and how I used it in conjunction with the stories in my data, a graduate student raised her hand and hotly contested my research topic:

> I just can't keep quiet anymore, are you trying to tell me you're using critical race theory and using it with illegal immigrants? Illegal immigrants broke the law. They chose to ignore the rules of our borders and come over here on their own free will. I just have a real problem with you using that theory and acting they should have any rights.

Her comment illustrates the argument that often is used to justify withholding resources from undocumented immigrants: These people broke the law, they made the choice, and now they must suffer the consequences. While this story is accurate insofar as people without official paperwork living in the United States technically are breaking laws, it does not explore the more detailed reality of why and how these people came to this country and why they remain. It is important to consider all of these questions more carefully as we consider this most recent history of migration to the United States.

While majoritarian stories often only frame the experience of migration with a more recent lens, the reality is that migration is a worldwide, historically reoccurring phenomenon. John, one of the teachers, illustrated this point well when he said,

> Migrations have happened throughout the history of humankind, for war or famine like the Irish, for national disasters like tsunamis or earthquakes or for economic deprivation and that's what we are seeing here. The forces of migration are beyond what people can do to stop it. I look at history and an example like China where people constructed a huge wall to keep people out, and it didn't keep anybody out. Because when people migrate, they are going to find a way to get in, to get over walls. They're going to get under walls, they're going to go through walls, and they're going to go around walls. You're not going to be able to stop them.

Mr. John, like many of the other teacher allies at the school, recognized the complexity of immigration issues, and emphasized that immigration to North Carolina was not a product of only personal decisions by Mexicans and other immigrants, but a product of capitalistic larger forces. John said, "The only way you can stop this migration is through the people who are really responsible for it." While many people are quick to place blame on and express anger with undocumented immigrants, Latino families came to Sunder Crossings in response to work opportunities at the large factory in town.[23]

Research documents that people have been recruited in small towns in Mexico, receiving phone calls from small towns in North Carolina asking that new workers be sent to cities in the state to do work at meat and poultry factories (Kandel & Parrado, 2004). Over the years, the connections from towns in Mexico to places like Sunder Crossings have grown into larger social networks. People have come in response to these social networks, to reunify family members and to survive given the poor working conditions in Mexico.

The story of immigration into North Carolina is one that may involve illegality, but everyone who lives in the state and the nation is implicit in this illegality. Mr. David, a teacher with a passion for social justice, had strong feelings about people who speak poorly of the undocumented immigrants, but have no problem accepting what benefits they receive from their presence in the United States work force:

---

[23] The majority of work available in the poultry and meat factories in North Carolina is low wage, and often work that residents of North Carolina refuse to take part in because the dangerous and unpleasant conditions.

> My favorite one is going into Wal-Mart and hearing the old
> ladies bitch about the fact that Mexicans need to speak
> English, and then buying the four dollar chicken. If you told
> those ladies, "Hey, no problem the chicken's going to cost
> eight dollars." They would stare at you like a moron. It never
> clicks. The benefits they are receiving from the way things
> are set up. And just the fact that we don't have a policy; we
> don't have a guest worker policy. We have a policy of very
> weak enforcement of labor laws. We see Latino workers
> getting hurt at a much higher rate than any other working
> group. They take the jobs that are really dangerous and then
> corporations don't enforce the safety regulations to begin with.

Other teachers at the school also recognized that the jobs that Latinos
worked in Sunder Crossings were undesirable to other residents. Stacey
lamented, "The jobs that Latinos do here in Sunder Crossings are the
ones that nobody wants. If you take them back and send them to their
native country, who is going to do all the jobs that no one wants to do?"

The story of immigration is complex, and the victims of the broken
immigration system are these students. Like other immigrants before
them, their families have come in response to work and in search of a
better life than (in a large number of cases) the poverty they left behind.
Stacey, who often argued with other teachers about undocumented
student and immigration issues, said,

> Then when I hear that argument "well, they just need to play
> by the rules," and I say, "who made the rules?" Everybody
> comes here, and they came here in the past and they come here
> now looking for better opportunities. Sometimes they will ask
> me directly, "what is your point of view," and I will say, "well
> if they've been here for five years and if they have been here
> since they were young, and they had no choice in the matter, I
> think that we should let them apply to college, and let them
> become legal."

Stacey's response is passionate, but it also poses important questions
that are not often brought to the forefront of the immigration debate.
Who did make the rules? The history of immigration law demonstrates
that racial preferences and discrimination have deeply influenced the
laws constructed. How did these children come to North Carolina?

They were brought here by their parents, who likely came for low-wage jobs that created a foundation for the U.S. economic backbone. Why should their children be allowed to go to college? We have made an investment in these children since they were young, and it makes sense to give them access to opportunity and to provide a path to legal citizenship. They have become resources that our nation should not squander. These important questions and discussion points often are left out of the heated debate that surrounds in-state tuition and immigration issues in North Carolina.

IN THEIR OWN WORDS

During the debate of House Bill 1183 (North Carolina's version of the DREAM Act), anti-immigrant groups made vocal outcry against giving undocumented students in-state tuition. These groups flooded the airways and wrote in to their local newspapers to spew their anti-immigrant, anti-Mexican rhetoric. Yet, the people who likely were to be most affected by an in-state tuition bill -- students who were undocumented -- were rarely heard from in the debate. Many of undocumented students at BGHS wanted to speak out in their schools, and in their communities but respect and fear for their families kept them from doing so. These students' voices were silenced in the process, and their invisibility maintained as a protective device. Nonetheless, they held fierce personal beliefs about why they should be granted access to higher education. It seems appropriate in this chapter on counterstories to let their voices, without analysis or interpretation, stand on their own:

> Carmen: I think we're all humans and if we have the capacity, to continue in school, but that's really hard (with current laws). I think that if a person really wants to be someone in the future, it doesn't matter if they are illegal or not, they should have the same opportunities I think that everybody who wants to do it should be able to finish their education.

> Fidel: I think I would like to tell others that it's not my fault. I was brought here by my parents. I didn't make the choice. I actually wrote an essay about it where I pretended to be the mastermind behind the whole thing (my parents coming here) and me getting into the U.S., and then at the very end I revealed that I was only nine years old. And the main

message was you cannot judge the person, the child was only nine years old.

Ricardo: I would tell them that if you want to go to college, that is a sign that you will be a productive member of society in some way.

Frances: I don't, like how do you say it in English, I don't know how to say it. Like they don't um, *aprovechar* (take advantage of) like they have it (the right to attend college) but they don't value it. Like a lot of Americans they can go to college, they have the opportunity, and they don't even take advantage of it. Well I think it's all just pretty unfair.

Saul: You know, that's really why I wanted to go to college, to go and learn and experience new things. I didn't really want to go to college just to make more money. I guess I wanted to get into college, just to see what college life was like. I want to experience different things and learn about different things in life. I think we should all have the opportunity if we also have the desire.

TRANSNATIONAL CAPITAL

Enrique Trueba's (Trueba, 2002; Trueba, 2004; Trueba & Bartolome) work explored the experience of transnational students. In his work, Trueba argued that these particular students had a unique capacity to live in different cultures, to master multiple languages, and to navigate multiple roles and relationships in American society. His research highlighted the strengths of the transnational students, including their knowledge and fluency in both English and Spanish and their full participation in both American and Mexican culture. Trueba wrote about transnational students' strong sense of ethnic affiliation and the strong ties they kept with their families and the culture of their country of origin. He argued that, based on these strengths, transnational students possess cultural capital that will soon be viewed as an invaluable cultural commodity. He contended that their ability to redefine themselves and to act as "border crossers" (Anzaldua, 1987) would some day put them ahead of their American counterparts.

The undocumented students at BGHS are exactly the sort of transnational students Trueba described. They are academically high achieving, fluent in Spanish and English, hard working (most held jobs outside of school), and act in multiple roles in their community. During their time in the United States, these undocumented students at Benson Guthrie High School have acted as translators for both their families and within the school system, as academic tutors for newcomer students, as activists for the local Latino outreach organization, and as dedicated athletes, church members, and sons and daughters. They are eager, motivated, intelligent, resilient, and resourceful. They are the type of students that teachers are eager to help in school (as one can tell from their teacher allies) and the type of college students professors would be eager to see enter into their classrooms in the fall.

The counterstories provided herein verify the academic capabilities, including intelligence, hard work, resourcefulness, and resilience, of the undocumented students at Benson Guthrie High School. These stories create a strong argument that transnational capital is lost when such undocumented students are not given access to continue their education beyond high school. The power of counterstory is the opportunity to show a different social reality built from the lived experiences of undocumented students. Providing these stories helps these undocumented students and others like them recognize that they are not alone on this journey. These stories challenge the deficit perspectives that people hold about what it means to be "illegal" and create a paradigmatic shift that teaches others the value and capability of the undocumented student. Ultimately, these stories, together with other counterstories about the undocumented student experience, have the potential to transform belief systems and construct new stories that define the undocumented student as a valuable and contributing member of society, a member worthy of more equitable treatment including the public benefits of higher education.

CHAPTER 9
The Policies of Wasted Potential

This book examined the experiences of undocumented, Mexican-immigrant students at Benson Guthrie High School in North Carolina, a state whose higher education policies deny in-state tuition for these students. The book addresses the scarcity of research on undocumented students living in states with such policies and to document the difficulty of accessing the college pipeline in those states. The data also informs our understanding of the lived experiences of undocumented students, the teachers and family members who care about them and the impact these policies have on North Carolina and the United States. This research provides evidence of how undocumented students who are prepared to attend college find themselves severely challenged because of their documentation status within a broken immigration system. Ultimately, this book provides support to the argument that, at a time when the U.S. needs more talented students with bicultural and bilingual abilities, the state of North Carolina is squandering its opportunity to utilize the resources of their undocumented student population.

The policies on undocumented immigrants accessing higher education are not race neutral. They are shaped by the history of immigration law (Motomura, 2006), which involved strict quotas on the number of Mexican immigrants coming into the United States

(Ngai, 2004), border patrol policies that were crafted specifically to keep "undesirable" Latino immigrants out of the country, and the label "illegal alien" constructed as a Mexican-origin identification (Nevins, 2002). The current in-state tuition policies in North Carolina perpetuate the racial subordination of Mexican-immigrant communities by preventing their educational advancement and by positioning them as less capable and less deserving than other students in the state.

The academic background including the coursework, the test scores and the involvement in the school community of these students demonstrated that they not only earned high school diplomas, but were prepared to begin college-level coursework, and to contribute to a campus community. While they did not have parents who were able to help them navigate the college application process, the teacher allies served as "institutional agents" (Stanton-Salazar, 2001) to college information for these children.

While these students have positioned themselves favorably for the college application process, the admission policies in the state made the process extremely difficult for them. The policies of UNC's 16-campus system, which require that undocumented students apply as out-of-state students, compete in the out-of-state student pool, and pay out-of-state tuition, do not represent any level of parity where access to education is concerned.[24] Community colleges' policies in the state also require undocumented students to pay out--of-state tuition. While public school perpetuates the myth that everyone is on equal footing and if someone just works hard enough, that person could make something of himself or herself, the policies for access to higher education, and for citizenship status, prohibit students from obtaining access to secure post-secondary opportunities.

These structurally deterministic (Delgado & Stefanic, 2001) policies left the teachers who worked with these students severely constrained in providing help to pursue realistic post-high school options. Because of the general immigration policies in the United States, many students also were unable to participate in successful programs in the high school such as the allied health and paid tutoring programs.

---

[24] Many selective, public universities have even higher admission standards in order to reduce the size of the pool that will be admitted from outside the state. For example, in 2005 the average SAT score of in-state students was 1288 for North Carolina freshmen and 1356 for out-of-state freshmen.

MULTIPLE CONTEXTS AND MULTIPLE IDENTITIES

This research supports previous research findings, which show the disconnect that often exists between immigrant students' homes and their schools (Suárez-Orozco & Suárez-Orozco, 2001; Valdes, 1998; Valenzuela, 1999). While all of the students managed to balance their academic identity with their transnational cultural identity, they did this with some level of tension. Parents supported their child's high school education, but many of them did not have higher education expectations for these students. The school, on the other hand, pushed for all of their students to work hard in order to be able to go to college. The differing expectations were not a result of the parents having lower expectations than the school, but of the parents' minimal experience with a college-going culture in their country of origin.

As these students tried to balance their academic and home identities, the data revealed that their "smart" identities positioned them in a protective space at school. As a result of their "smart" identity, they all were encouraged to pursue higher education, but this was not the case for their undocumented classmates who were in regular, ESL, or remedial coursework. For these students, the "smart identity" allowed them to pass successfully through the educational pipeline up until they made attempts to access college. At that point they came up against concrete barriers of policies and laws that relegated them to a second-class level of citizenship, that of an "illegal immigrant." These moments not only revealed the "myth of the meritocracy," but exposed the reality of a status-dependent meritocracy.

Yet, data also support that rather than being positioned by society as "illegal immigrants," students were beginning to craft their new identity as "undocumented" persons (Solis, 2004; Solis, 2005). While this new identity resulted in college attendance for one of the students, the other students had to continue to position themselves into spaces where they could live by their own definitions rather than those with which society had labeled them. The students' multiple and often conflicting identities suggest that the invisibility of "undocumented status" at BGHS serves as both a protection for the students and a missed opportunity for the teachers to prepare these students for real life outside the high school walls.

TACTICS OF RESISTANCE

While these students at BGHS had favorable positions as "smart students," at least one student experienced discrimination because of her Mexican-immigrant background. Frances' narrative regarding her academic transcripts demonstrates that educational inequities occurred with the immigrant student population that arrived to Sunder Crossings. The data also revealed that despite, or perhaps because of, the obstacles placed in front of them, the students displayed differing forms of resistance (de Certau, 1984; Scott, 1990; Solórzano & Delgado-Bernal, 2001). With self-defeating resistance, undocumented students dropped out of high school; through conformist resistance, students did well inside the school system to prove that they could succeed despite their undocumented status; and using transformative resistance, students not only expressed verbal criticism of the immigration system in the United States, but also took active steps against it by organizing students to participate in an immigration rally challenging the current system.

Some students displayed forms of resistance not identified in previous research (Solórzano & Yosso, 2002; Yosso, 2006). Students objected that "success" after high school should be so narrowly defined by whether or not one accesses the higher education pipeline, and argued that providing for one's family is an essential mark of success. They also believed learning did not occur only within the confines of the traditional education systems in the United States. While the students succeeded in school despite the obstacles placed in front of them, and redefined what a happy and successful life might be for each of them, they displayed a form of resistance I named *transnational resilient resistance*. This resistance is deeply rooted in the experiences of the undocumented Mexican-immigrant students in this research.

This research expands the understanding of forms of resistance, and also supports past research (Solórzano & Delgado-Bernal, 2001; Solórzano & Yosso, 2002; Yosso, 2006) showing that undocumented students living with intersecting oppressions, including immigration status, race, class and language, do not fit into one single category of oppression, nor do they respond with one category of resistance behavior.

COUNTERSTORIES

Although negative majoritarian stories (Solórzano & Yosso, 2002) created narratives of rejection, the undocumented students' lives themselves created powerful counternarratives to challenge those deficit perspectives. While anti-immigrant and anti-Mexican sentiment perpetuated by majoritarian stories positions undocumented students as "problems" and undeserving of in-state tuition, the lives of these students at BGHS reveal the great assets these students would provide not only to universities but the global marketplace as well.

The counterstories constructed by the undocumented students and the teachers allies demonstrate that these students have "earned" their place at universities by the hard work, intelligence, and resourcefulness shown throughout their high school careers. The students' and parents' lives represent a counternarrative to the often widely accepted belief that immigrants choose to come here on their own free will, and then drain state resources. Their stories complicate the discussion on immigration, on the broken immigration system, and on how people feel toward undocumented immigrants in the school systems. Finally, the lives of these students reveal that the state is missing an opportunity to capitalize on the transnational capital that these students bring to their communities and to North Carolina. Each day the state continues to prevent access to higher education is a day that the state loses out on the economic and social benefits of this transnational student population.

POLICIES OF WASTED POTENTIAL

The implications of keeping college-ready undocumented students from receiving in-state tuition and thus creating near to impossibility of attending four-year universities bear on the interests of all North Carolinians and all Americans. By encouraging a college-age population in the state, individuals with higher degrees will earn higher incomes, thus strengthening the tax revenue and economic activity in the state. The more educated a state's population, the fewer demands they place on social services, including the welfare system and prison systems. This lessening demand costs the state fewer dollars than uneducated populations, which require more of these public services. It is simply in the interest of the state to educate as many students as possible, especially those populations with little history of access to higher education. Finally, the more educated a state is, the more well-prepared it is to handle decisions about health care, personal finance, and retirement. Again, the result would be less expense to the state because it would not have to take responsibility for those areas in people's personal lives. Creating an easily accessible and high quality higher education system is vital to states' accruing the benefits of a population that generates tax revenues rather than expands them (National Center Public Policy Report, 2004). In other words, creating access to undocumented students, through an in-state tuition policy, should be an integral part of North Carolina and other similarly anti-immigrant states' strategic plans for building the most highly educated population possible.

To create such a population, college-ready undocumented students in North Carolina should have access to higher education through legislation that creates full support for both a state and federal level DREAM Act bill. Such a proposed law in North Carolina would involve a comprehensive student adjustment bill, which would include not only access to in-state tuition but also a well-detailed path to citizenship status in the United States. Without such a path the state will not have the opportunity to benefit from the transnational capital the students provide because undocumented students, even though college-educated, will find themselves unable to work after graduation. Without a path to citizenship, undocumented students face yet another level of institutionalized racism once they graduated from university. By allowing students to attend college and to follow a path to citizenship, North Carolina would be able to create a stronger educational capital base than currently exists in the state.

In order to increase access to both the public and private education systems, four-year universities should adopt more aggressive and flexible admission policies for college-ready undocumented students. While UNC's16-campus system should be applauded for adopting a clear and well-defined admission policy regarding undocumented students, the current guidelines do not create any level of parity for these academically prepared students. If undocumented students can prove that they have attended a North Carolina high school for all four years, they should be allowed to compete in the in-state student pool. While North Carolina currently prohibits access to state and federal aid, the state should take the lead from other large immigrant-receiving states such as Texas and make available state aid for those students who qualify as residents (i.e. students who can prove they have been in the state for at least four years, and that it is their fixed and permanent residency).[25] This group of students could be considered as "special

---

[25] Students who can show that they have been in the country for more than four years would alleviate fears that students from Mexico will come streaming over the borders if they think in-state tuition is available to anyone who applies to a North Carolina university. If students can demonstrate that they have attended a North Carolina high school for four years, they also likely will be able to demonstrate that their family has been living and contributing to the North Carolina economy for that period of time as well. Because of strict border enforcement we can assume that these immigrant student families, which already have lived in the state for at least four years, view North Carolina as their fixed abode.

cases" similar to many other groups (including military personnel and family of faculty and staff) who apply to the university.

From a policy standpoint, those who believe money would be lost by allowing undocumented students' in-state tuition should urge more comprehensive studies on high school graduation and dropout rates in the state. Policy groups such as the Education Trust, argue that North Carolina's graduation rates, which are reported as quite high, and the state's dropout rates, which are reported as quite low, particularly for Latino students, are grossly misrepresented (Adams, 2005). Judging by the anecdotal evidence of dropping out at BGHS, a resistance strategy practiced by undocumented students, the state should consider how much it costs the state when undocumented student does not finish high school. Both dropout and graduation rate reports should be interrogated for their accuracy. As scholars (Suárez-Orozco and Suárez-Orozco, 2001) have argued in the past, the implications of not providing higher education to undocumented immigrant students is likely to be more costly than providing in-state benefits.

The current reality also solicits practical recommendations for the state until a comprehensive DREAM Act is passed. These policy recommendations, while not the preferable solution, would create at least some level of sensitivity and helpfulness towards teachers, parents and adults working with undocumented children living in North Carolina.

The first recommendation is for the state of North Carolina to demand that a comprehensive policy manual about the admission policies for undocumented students be developed and disseminated at each public and private university, within the community college system, and at each high school in the state. This policy manual could be modeled after the *College and Financial Aid Guide for AB540 Undocumented Immigrant Students in California* (Oliverez, Chavez, Soriano, & Tierney, 2006).

During the research process it became obvious that few public or private universities in the state made their admission guidelines easily accessible. My difficulty in finding information was echoed by the many high school counselors and teachers I met working with undocumented students throughout the state. Therefore, a comprehensive manual that would include the admission guidelines (including a definition of common terms used in the application process), the tuition prices and the federal laws regarding the issue, would be immensely helpful for school personnel across the state. In addition, a listing of national scholarships available to students regardless of citizenship, as well as a listing of advocacy groups across the state and nation (including the North Carolina Society for Hispanic Professionals, El Pueblo Inc, the Mexican American Legal Defense Fund, etc.) could be included in this guide. Such a guide should be made available as a tool not only for high schools, but also in college admission offices statewide. Preferably, the guide would be available in both English and Spanish.

College admission offices across North Carolina also should develop more culturally sensitive practices for working with undocumented students. The current application process requires students to share their undocumented status in the public arena. The undocumented students in the research had a great degree of difficulty in filling out the international student application (i.e. how do applicants provide their "home" addresses in Mexico, or their parents' occupations in Mexico), or answering questions in phone interviews from admission staff who believed they were speaking to international students. Admission offices should develop a process that identifies to the admission staff whether they are working with an "international" student who lives in North Carolina and, consequently, should be sensitive to questions that may make this student uncomfortable or even fearful. Universities need not lower their academic standards for undocumented students but they should take into account that the first language spoken in a child's family likely is not English; thus, standardized test scores and essays should be carefully evaluated against the advantages afforded to an English-dominant child born and raised in the United States.

When reviewing extracurricular activities, admission offices should consider whether or not undocumented students may be expected to work to provide income for their families, and whether or not they are expected to stay home and take care of other family members while their parents work. Whenever possible, universities also should consider what type of receiving environment an immigrant student has experienced at school. If schools have not made concrete attempts to integrate and make welcome immigrant students, the children, just like their parents, may feel uncomfortable being involved in the high school. This discomfort may be reflected in their lack of extracurricular activities at school.

The state is losing out on the transnational capital possessed by undocumented students. Research conducted on the economic impact of Hispanics living in the state (Kasarda & Johnson, 2006), should be expanded in North Carolina to gather more evidence about the net economic gain from the impact of Hispanics around the state. Such reports should carefully outline anticipated economic gains produced as a result of global partnerships secured with the help of a potential transnational work force. Such a work force in North Carolina would be led by the undocumented student population.

IMPLICATIONS FOR PRACTICE: BUILDING COLLEGE PREP PROGRAMS FOR UNDOCUMENTED STUDENTS

Throughout the research process, I worked as a director of a small mentoring and college preparatory program serving Latino immigrant students at BGHS. This program was multilayered to encourage academic excellence and increase college-going rates for the Latino students involved. When the program was created, we were interested in serving all of the Latino students at the high school; thus, we made the decision to accept applications for the program regardless of citizenship status. This decision created unique challenges. We did not ask whether students were U.S. citizens or undocumented immigrants, but by building trusting relationships, we came to understand that approximately half of students in each class (the program began in a student's sophomore year) were not U.S. citizens. Building this program over the past three years resulted in some successes and some failures, but as this program and others like it continue to grow, we can learn more each year how better to meet the needs of the Latino students from varying generational and citizenship backgrounds. The following list of key elements for the mentoring/college prep program, can be used as guidelines for college campuses that seek to create such programs in new immigrant-serving communities.

> 1. <u>Involve the parents</u>. Immigrant parents are not always familiar with the school culture and are even less so with the college-going culture of the high school. Still, when given the chance, they are eager to learn and participate in their children's lives. Making them feel welcome by having a translator available or holding events off school grounds was extremely effective at BGHS. We also encouraged all of the family members to come to events, when appropriate. While the parents of some of the undocumented students in this research did not particularly esteem higher education, college prep programs should work with the assumption that most parents will be involved if you make a sustained effort to educate them as well as their children in the process. In addition,

parents serve as great outreach networks to communicate and educate others parents and students about the college preparatory and application process.

2. <u>Make relevant information easily available to students and their families</u>. Explain relevant information carefully. While you may think that students are receiving the same information regarding college applications, SAT/ACT deadlines, and scholarship opportunities, remember that first-generation Latino students are the first in their families to go to college. This means that no one is at home explaining how the college application process works. Basic vocabulary and step by step tutorials for both parents and their students make the process much less intimidating.

3. <u>Find mentors who can speak Spanish.</u> While college students with Latino backgrounds serve as excellent role models for these programs, finding any mentor (regardless of ethnic background) who fluently can speak Spanish and can communicate with the parents of the student in their native language is an added benefit. Spanish speaking mentors can serve as a bridge between home and school.

4. <u>Create an environment that creates high expectations and consistently reinforces the academic and cultural identity of the student.</u> Past research supports that a college-going culture may be absent in ESL and general education courses where Latino immigrants often are overrepresented (Erisman & Looney, 2007, Oliverez, 2005). In the Latino Outreach program, we worked hard to set a high academic bar (in terms of honors and AP coursework) for all students, and then to create scaffolds (Mehan, 1994; Moll & Ruiz, 2002) to reach those bars. These scaffolds included not only the mentors themselves, but also academic tutoring available in the school to help students reach the personal goals set with their mentors. The program also supported the transnational value of the home environment by inviting parents to come in and learn with the students and by encouraging maintenance and enhancement of the Spanish language (the school offered an AP Spanish course and one course in Spanish for native speakers). The program tried to create a bridge between academic and cultural identities of students involved in the program.

5. <u>Be honest with the students regarding their college options</u>. Building a program with undocumented students involves difficult conversations regarding the current policies and laws especially in states that have no tuition equity legislation, but these conversations are necessary. Undocumented students must understand that it will be significantly more difficult for them to be admitted to university and to find funding than for their U.S. citizen peers. This difficult conversation must occur early in the program. It makes no sense to be dishonest about the laws and policies. Thus, a conversation that lays out the obstacles and makes a pledge of support to help the student in every way possible is crucial when planning for the future.

6. <u>When possible secure funding from outside sources</u>. When we began our program, only one Latino scholarship was available in the state for students, regardless of citizenship status in North Carolina. Thus, we searched for an organization that would host a scholarship and would work around undocumented immigration status. Making connections with advocacy groups in the community was important in finding such an organization. After our second year, we were able to secure an organization to "host" our scholarship; luckily, this was a well-known, large nonprofit association in the state. Although it is not yet a large endowment, this scholarship opportunity provides tangible incentives for the students who are working in the program.

7. <u>Expose students to college life as much as possible.</u> Since most our students were recent immigrants, their familiarity with college life and college campuses was little to none. Bringing them to college campuses, having them participate in activities and events on campus as much as possible, and having them interact with college students reinforces the message that they belong there as well. Staying in the dorms, showing students how to use the library, bringing them and their families to events on campus helps eliminate fears of the unknown.

8. <u>Create individual plans according to the options available</u>. While a general college preparatory curriculum may serve a large audience as a "one size fits all" plan, using one-on-one or small group mentoring team creates an environment for individual plans to be created and executed. In our program, the range of Latino

students in one senior class included legal permanent residents, undocumented students, and U.S. citizens; thus, it was necessary to make individual college application plans according to the needs and the lived realities of the students involved. While the goal of our program was attendance at a four-year university, the program also encouraged community college when financial obstacles prohibited an undocumented student from attendance at a four-year university. Transferring from a two-year to a four-year institution was included in the college plan for these students.

9. <u>Create flexibility for students needs</u>. Many of the Latino students in our program had financial responsibilities to their families, which included working and contributing to their households or babysitting for siblings while their parents worked. Each semester we tried to make event planning for the program as flexible as possible (only academic events were absolutely mandatory) by organizing events during days and at times the students most likely were to be available (generally weekends and directly after school worked best). The program also had tutors who volunteered in the school so that students could receive help, during school hours, with their classroom work.

10. <u>Recognize that Latino immigrants are not a homogenous group</u>. Within the Latino immigrant Diaspora your program may be serving students from different cultures (even within the same countries of origin), education levels, socioeconomic and citizenship status. Individual students will have varied levels of English language proficiency ranging from English as their first language, to newly arrived immigrants who are just beginning to learn English. In addition, their families' experiences with public education and higher education (both in their families' country of origin and in the United States) will vary as well. Taking time to learn about the diversity within the program displays an authentic sense of care and will help ultimately build a stronger program.

11. <u>Make yourself a presence in the community as much as possible, and as much as the school will allow.</u> Encourage mentors involved in the program to spend time in the school and in the community, and provide organized activities for them to do so. In our case, college mentors were able to set up volunteer tutoring hours in the school and also take a service-learning course at the

university that had placements within the school and with other community organizations in the area. When mentors spent time in the school for structured tutoring events, they often stayed after school to watch sports events and to volunteer their time with after-school activities. The genuine interest in the school created closer relationships with the mentees and more accountability for both parties.

The Latino Outreach Program was able to utilize the resources of the university and to establish a presence in the school (although the school managed and limited this presence); however, in order to advocate for undocumented students, unconventional institutions and organizations may work best with the particular difficult circumstances faced by such students. Often these nonprofit organizations, such as the Hispanic advocacy/liaison center in Sunder Crossings, are willing to advocate for more progressive policies without fear of government or state reprimand. Often, these organizations also are immigrant-run and offer undocumented immigrants information without being exposed as non-citizens. Such groups use the "cracks" in the system (de Certau, 1984) to subvert the current laws and policies and to create the types of social justice agendas that allow people to develop an "undocumented" versus "illegal" reality (Solis, 2004, 2005). Whenever possible, as activist scholars we must pledge time and commitments to organizations such as these.

THE POSSIBILITIES TO RECAPTURE LOST TALENT

The policies and laws surrounding undocumented high school students change slowly, but they do, in fact, change. In 2001, no states had in-state tuition policies for undocumented students; now 10 states have such a law. A federal law would be the most effective means to create a uniform system; event without it, however, higher education and immigration advocates have chipped away at state policies, and with a significant amount of success. Even so, each day without an in-state tuition policy is another day that a gifted undocumented student is unable to continue his or her education, an education earned like their North Carolina peers.

While I do not wish to generalize the experiences of these undocumented students to represent all undocumented students, I do hope this book contributes to the understanding of the great loss of talent that is occurring when a state fails to recognize the transnational capital that is lost by prohibiting realistic admission and tuition policies for undocumented students. Because of their academic identity, these students were able to remain resilient through the K-12 process, but the graduation and dropout rates for other Latino students in the state, many of whom are undocumented high school students, indicate that daily assaults on their values as a person greatly affect their chances for high school completion.

As a CRT and LatCrit scholar committed to social justice and praxis, I offer this book and the work of the Latino Outreach group as a contribution to what we understand about the undocumented student experience, and what we can do to help these students overcome the obstacles placed in front of them. The structurally deterministic policies do not make this easy for any of the children or those of us who are committed to these students, but students such as Fidel demonstrate that it is not completely impossible to attend college in a state that has no tuition equity policies. While the anti-immigrant, anti-Mexican sentiment does not create an optimistic outlook that laws and policies will soon change in North Carolina or even nationwide, I survive on the hope created by these undocumented students who continue to dream a better life for themselves and their families.

Epilogue

Nearly four years after the students received their high school diplomas only one of the five undocumented students will walk across another stage in May to receive a college diploma. Despite their academic preparation and their motivation to succeed, the policies in North Carolina continue to create significant barriers to access higher education.

The University of North Carolina System continues to uphold its policy, established in 2004, which allows undocumented students to apply to college as out-of-state students. No federal or state financial aid is offered to these students. In December 2007 the University of North Carolina's Tomorrow Commission released recommendations on how to respond more proactively to 21st century challenges facing North Carolina. Among the recommendations was that the university system examine strategies to determine possible circumstances when academically-qualified undocumented students should be charged in-state tuition. To date the UNC system has taken no steps to make in-state tuition available to undocumented students.

In spring of 2009 the North Carolina Community College (Lee et al., 2009) released a study on the admission of undocumented students into the North Carolina Community College System. After nearly 10 years of flip-flopping on both system wide and individual college policies, the report recommended that NCCS pursue a statewide admission policy mandating that all members of the NCCS system admit undocumented students at out-of-state tuition rates. The report documented that the current UNC system policy creates little added cost or burden to their institutions and that allowing undocumented students to be admitted and pay out-of-state tuition creates no taxpayer burden for higher education costs. In fact, requiring undocumented students to pay out-of-state tuition would create revenue for the North Carolina Community College System.

In September of 2009, and in recognition of the report, the 21-member NCCC board voted to solidify a policy that allows undocumented students to attend all North Carolina Community Colleges if they are able to pay the out of state tuition. In essence, both the UNC system and the NCCS now have official policies that continue to maintain the status quo. Sadly, both of these small and hollow victories could be overturned in the spring if, as some legislators have threatened, the North Carolina General Assembly debates bills that, like South Carolina, expressly forbid all undocumented students from accessing any type of higher education in the state.

As North Carolina continues to ignore the global commodity of its transnational student population, the undocumented students from BGHS have all in some way, shape or form struggled to access higher education. After graduation, Carmen continued to work at a local fast-food restaurant and helped as a volunteer coach for the girls' high school soccer team. She took a few community college courses at a nearby college, but the out-of- state tuition made attending full time prohibitive. A year after graduation, Carmen was accepted at a private Baptist university in Texas, where she received scholarship dollars to attend. She spent one year at the college and then dropped out due to the financial expenses and lack of financial aid. Upon returning to North Carolina, she moved to a town nearby Sunder Crossings. She is now a young mother and wife, and would consider returning to college if North Carolina would ever create such an opportunity.

While Carmen has remained close to home, Frances the other female student continues to live in Mexico. Directly after high school, Frances returned to Mexico in hopes of being adopted by her aunt and uncle (who were legal residents in Sunder Crossings) and legalizing her status back in the U.S. Staying first in a small town in Guerrero, Frances became bored quickly and moved to Mexico City to look for work. In Mexico City she worked as a bilingual receptionist for an Indian company, and then was promoted to an executive in charge of government sales. After working for six months, she became unsatisfied and left the company in 2007 to return to college. Hearing little from North Carolina about the possibilities to legalize her status, she began attending the Universidad Autonoma Metropolina de México (UAM). Working part time and attending school part time proved difficult and after less than a year, she dropped out of UAM.

In December 2008, Frances and her brother were given an appointment with the U.S. Consulate in Cuidad Juarez. The trip to Juarez was expensive, including the travel to and from Mexico City, a medical exam and time in hotels while they awaited their interviews. It is unclear exactly why, but Frances' brother was able to obtain his passport and return to North Carolina through the adoption process as a legal resident, but because of her strained relationship with her aunt and uncle, Frances must provide her own finances to obtain her passport and travel to the U.S. consulate in North Carolina. Currently, she works as a receptionist for a large company in Mexico City. She is unsure if she will be able to save enough money to return to the United States in time to make a 2009 deadline for the U.S. consulate paperwork. She feels unclear whether she has any interest in returning to the U.S. because of the way Latinos are treated, always she says as a "minor class and nothing more."

The young men in the research have faced different obstacles, as well as opportunities since graduation day. For Saul, the young man who felt a strong responsibility to his family, a welding job took him to several different places around the United States; locations that helped him recognize that he didn't want to be so far from family and home. Several months after graduation, Saul returned to North Carolina to work locally in the area. For several years he worked and helped support his family. Saul remained close to the soccer team he had led to a state victory in high school, as well as with teachers at the school.

In 2007, deciding that higher education was still important, Saul began saving up money in the summer to attend college. Through professional contacts at different universities, Saul and other friends found that one historically black college/university (HBCU) in the local area was receptive to increasing the ethnic diversity of its student body. While still not able to offer in-state tuition, Saul and other students found this college to be a welcome community for Latino immigrant students. Currently, Saul works full time in the summers in order to help pay for his tuition at this HBCU and aspires to graduate in 2011. In addition to taking care of his immediate family, he now also takes care of a family of his own. Saul and his wife (another student who was a legal immigrant in the Latino Outreach program) have a newborn son. Both Saul and his wife attend college together and commute back and forth to Sunder Crossings where they live with their family who help raise their son.

Fidel, the BGHS academic superstar of the high school will complete his college degree from a highly selective university in the fall of 2009. Supported by private scholarships, which have paid for his entire college experience, Fidel will complete his English degree in four years. The entire experience has been a roller coaster. A ride that has included feeling fear and anger when anti-immigration students groups have invited politicians such as former U.S. Senator Tom Tancredo to campus to speak, working as a mentor in the Latino Outreach program and seeing two of his mentees graduate and attend college, and continuing his outward forms of resistance by keeping an active blog on his experiences in the academy as an undocumented student.

In the fall of his senior year, the future is unknown. The options he thinks about include continuing on to graduate school (but without a funder such as he had in undergraduate, this seems unlikely), figuring out if a company or organization is willing to look the other way where documentation is concerned and hire him, or returning to Mexico (both of his parents have indicated that they would like to return, and while he can't imagine life back in Mexico, he also can't imagine life here in the US without any family). His dream: to become an English teacher in the United States.

Through the entire experience, Fidel comments that it is the little things that have been the most difficult. While many might believe it is the big, unique opportunities that are out of reach because of his status, such as studying abroad or getting to attend an alternative spring break, which haven't been easy either, it's the small, taken for granted everyday experiences of a college student that are sometimes the hardest. Fear of driving around in a car (even as only a passenger because he does not drive without a license), because the fear of being stopped by the police makes even a quick trip to the store, to the movies or to another city to attend an event a pulse-racing and worrisome experience for an undocumented student. These are the hardest moments Fidel remarks, when you'd like to think you're an everyday college kid in a T-shirt and jeans, but you are constantly reminded that you are less than as compared to your college peers.

Finally, the student who had disappeared into the shadows in response to his legal problems (providing false documentation while working as a tutor at the high school), has resurfaced in a most amazing way. Ricardo, who had slipped off the radar of the teachers at the school following high school graduation, reappeared at BGHS in 2008. After working "here and there" for nearly three years, Ricardo returned to visit Ms. Stacey (a teacher ally) to see if there were any options to attend college. In a moment of incredibly good timing, the Latino Outreach program had established a new partnership with a selective out-of state university, which was interested in increasing its Latino student population and, in particular, willing to recruit undocumented students. Ms. Stacey connected Ricardo to the Latino Outreach program director and in the fall of 2009, because of his strong academic record, Ricardo became one of five undocumented students accepted (on full ride scholarships) and enrolled at this out-of-state university.

As a first-year student Ricardo believes that although by law he is still an undocumented student, the university treats him as an international student and in his everyday life he feels as though he is treated as a regular U.S. student by his peers. Sadly, while Ricardo will benefit from this incredible new partnership, he will be one of the only students to do so. Citing financial distress in a downturn economy, the private university, which at first indicated it would accept and provide scholarships each year for undocumented students, now has reneged on this promise and will only fund a few more students in fall 2010 before discontinuing the program at the end of next year.

While all the students want to attend and complete college, few students have hope that North Carolina state policies will change anytime soon, nor are they convinced that they (even if they became legal citizens) would be selected for work over a U.S.- born American peer. In such a fickle and downturn economy, Ricardo posits that undocumented college students may provide a solution. "Who's to the say the minds that will propel this country into the great days of prosperity once again are not the ones who are denied the chance?" At a very basic level all of the students believe it plain and simple, a waste of resources.

The students also continue to display forms of transnational resilient resistance by arguing that college is not a necessary tool for success. This perspective, that college is the only way, Ricardo notes in an email to me between his classes is a "Perspective that keeps many "uneducated" but smart immigrants from achieving positions where they can truly make a difference in the world." I would argue both sides of the coin -- that college isn't the only road to success, but that prohibiting access to college for undocumented immigrants also subordinates our immigrant students from achieving positions that can help make change.

As these students continue on their journeys, the Latino Outreach Program that worked with each of them at BGHS continues to prepare immigrant high school students for academic success in high school and beyond. At BGHS, the Latino student body continues to grow, now representing nearly 42 percent of the high school student body. The Outreach Program, which was started in 2003, has now mentored more than 60 Latino high school students and has grown to encompass four high schools throughout the state. The program has helped students gain admission to more than 12 different four-year colleges both in and out of North Carolina, and has helped Latino immigrant students, both citizens and undocumented, attend college. In addition, the Outreach Program serves as an advocate for increasing access to higher education for undocumented students, and provides leadership opportunities for Latino students to help create change in the future.

In 2008, the United States elected its first African-American president. Democratic President Barack Obama campaigned throughout his election year in support of the DREAM Act legislation to allow undocumented college students to attend college for in-state tuition and to create a path to citizenship in the process. During his first year in office Obama has prioritized the reform of health care as his No. 1 concern. Currently, at the end of 2009 it does not appear that comprehensive immigration reform or the DREAM Act on its own will be addressed in the near future. In absence of federal policy or official state legislation it is likely that the university and community college systems in North Carolina will continue to uphold a policy that creates no parity for undocumented students.

In 2009, Stella Flores and Catherine Horn (2009) published the first research on undocumented students attending a highly selective public college. Their research (which only re-emphasized what many educators who work with these students already knew) demonstrates that undocumented students at the University of Texas-Austin are remaining in college at the same rates as their Latino peers who are U.S. citizens and legal residents. Despite the hurdles, college-ready undocumented students, when given an equitable chance, succeed. Making successful education outcomes for undocumented students less an exception to the rule and more often the norm should from an economic, moral and social standpoint be an ongoing public policy priority.

APPENDIX A: CONSENT FORMS
University of X
Assent to Participate in a Research Study
Adolescent Participants age 15-17
Social Behavioral Form

IRB Study #_______05-043________________
Assent Form Version Date: _12/05/2005________________

Title of Study: Latino Trajectories Toward Higher Education

Principal Investigator: Janet Lopez
University Department: School of Education
University Phone Number Phone number:
Email Address:
Faculty Advisor:

Study Contact telephone number:
Study Contact email:

What are some general things you should know about research studies?

You are being asked to take part in a research study. Your parent, or guardian, needs to give permission for you to be in this study. You do not have to be in this study if you don't want to, even if your parent has already given permission. To join the study is voluntary. You may refuse to join, or you may withdraw your consent to be in the study, for any reason, without penalty.

Research studies are designed to obtain new knowledge. This new information may help people in the future. You may not receive any direct benefit from being in the research study. There also may be risks to being in research studies.

Details about this study are discussed below. It is important that you understand this information so that you can make an informed choice about being in this research study. You will be given a copy of this consent form. You should ask the researchers named above, or staff members who may assist them, any questions you have about this study at any time.

What is the purpose of this study?
This purpose of this research study is learn about the various contexts under which Latino students come to understand the pathway to college. This study will explore the perceptions of college and the directions which lead Latino students to access higher education. This study will explore the life experiences of higher education trajectories of different Latino students in North Carolina. You are being asked to participate in this study because you are a Latino student.

How many people will take part in this study?
If you decide to be in this study, you will be one of approximately one of 25 people in this research study.

How long will your part in this study last?
This study will be conducted during both your junior and senior year of high school. During this time you will be observed in your high school and in your home and local community approximately three times a year. You will be notified of these visits at least two weeks in advance. There will also be two in-depth interviews, one conducted during your junior year and one conducted during your senior year.

What will happen if you take part in the study?
- I would like permission to have a copy of your high school transcripts and your SAT and ACT test scores
- I would like permission to observe you and take fieldnotes in your high school, during after school activities and in your home several times during the school year.
- I would like to interview you about your thoughts about college during your junior year and again during your senior year. These interviews will include questions about your family background, your ideas about college, and your experiences in high school. Interviews will last approximately 2 hours.
- If you decide to participate in this study please understand that your participation is voluntary and that you have the right to withdraw your consent of discontinue participation at any time. You have the right to refuse to answer questions for any reason. In

addition you individual privacy will be maintained in all published and written data resulting from the study.

<u>What are the possible benefits from being in this study?</u>
Research is designed to benefit society by gaining new knowledge. You may also expect to benefit by participating in this study by gaining the opportunity to reflect on your feelings toward your experiences with learning and the college application process

<u>What are the possible risks or discomforts involved from being in this study?</u>
The risks involved in this study for you involve possible discomfort or embarrassment about questions that may asked about your interactions with your family and friends. I will do everything possible to minimize any discomfort you have concerning the questions asked during the interview. There may be uncommon or previously unknown risks. You should report any problems to the researcher.

<u>How will your privacy be protected?</u>
If you decide to participate in this study please understand that your participation is voluntary and that you have the right to withdraw your consent of discontinue participation at any time. You have the right to refuse to answer questions for any reason. In addition you individual privacy will be maintained in all published and written data resulting from the study. Participants' names will be replaced with pseudonyms in any and all write-ups. Taped interviews will be the property of the researcher, secured in a locked cabinet, and destroyed at the end of the project. Teachers and peers may be aware that you are involved in a study regarding how students understand college.

Participants will not be identified in any report or publication about this study. Although every effort will be made to keep research records private, there may be times when federal or state law requires the disclosure of such records, including personal information. This is very unlikely, but if disclosure is ever required, University X will take steps allowable by law to protect the privacy of personal information. In some cases, your information in this research study could be reviewed by representatives of the University, research sponsors, or government agencies for purposes such as quality control or safety.

Will you receive anything for being in this study?

For taking part in this study you will have the opportunity to utilize the principal investigator who is also a former college admission counselor. During your junior and senior year you will be able to utilize the principal investigator for help with the college admission and financial aid process. You will be able to utilize the primary researcher's help through email or phone consultation throughout the college process.

What if you have questions about this study?

You have the right to ask, and have answered, any questions you may have about this research. If you have questions, or concerns, you should contact the researchers listed on the first page of this form.

What if you have questions about your rights as a research participant?

All research on human volunteers is reviewed by a committee that works to protect your rights and welfare. If you have questions or concerns about your rights as a research subject you may contact, anonymously if you wish, the Institutional Review Board at XXX-XXX-XXXX or by email to IRB_subjects@edu.

----------- **Participant's Agreement:**

I have read the information provided above. I have asked all the questions I have at this time. I voluntarily agree to participate in this research study.

____

____
Your signature if you agree to be in the study   Date

____
Printed name if you agree to be in the study

____

____
Signature of Person Obtaining Assent   Date

University of X
Consent to Participate in a Research Study
Adult Participants
Social Behavioral Form

IRB Study #___05-043______________
Consent Form Version Date: _____12/05/2005__________

IRB Study #______05-043_____________
Assent Form Version Date: _12/05/2005____________

Title of Study: Latino Trajectories Toward Higher Education

Principal Investigator: Janet Lopez
University Department: School of Education
University Phone Number Phone number:
Email Address:
Faculty Advisor:

Study Contact telephone number:

<u>What are some general things you should know about research studies?</u>
You are being asked to take part in a research study. To join the study is voluntary.
You may refuse to join, or you may withdraw your consent to be in the study, for any reason, without penalty.

Research studies are designed to obtain new knowledge. This new information may help people in the future. You may not receive any direct benefit from being in the research study. There also may be risks to being in research studies.

Details about this study are discussed below. It is important that you understand this information so that you can make an informed choice about being in this research study.

You will be given a copy of this consent form. You should ask the researchers named above, or staff members who may assist them, any questions you have about this study at any time.

What is the purpose of this study?

This purpose of this research study is learn about the various contexts under which Latino students come to understand the pathway to college. This study will explore the perceptions of college and the directions which lead Latino students to access higher education. This study will explore the life experiences of higher education trajectories of different Latino students in North Carolina. You are being asked to be in the study because you are an adult who has a relationship with one of the youth participants who is the primary focus of this study.

How many people will take part in this study?

If you decide to be in this study, you will be one of approximately one of 25 people in this research study.

How long will your part in this study last?

This study will be conducted during the youth participants' junior and senior year of high school. During this time you may be observed in the high school or in your home with your student (this applies only to family members). Your primary participation in this study will include a tape-recorded interview.

What will happen if you take part in the study?

- I would like permission to observe you and take fieldnotes in the high school, during after school activities (this applies only to teachers and high school staff)
- I would like permission to observe you and take fieldnotes in your home (this applies to youth participant family members only)
- I would like to interview you about your thoughts about how Latino students pass through the college pipeline. These interviews may include questions about your own family background, your ideas about college, and your experiences with high school students. Interviews will last approximately 1 hour.
- If you decide to participate in this study please understand that your participation is voluntary and that you have the right to withdraw your consent of discontinue participation at any time. You have the right to refuse to answer questions for any reason. In

addition you individual privacy will be maintained in all published and written data resulting from the study.

What are the possible benefits from being in this study?

Research is designed to benefit society by gaining new knowledge. You may also expect to benefit by participating in this study by gaining the opportunity to reflect on your feelings toward your experiences with learning and the college application process.

What are the possible risks or discomforts involved from being in this study?

The risks involved in this study for you involve possible discomfort or embarrassment about questions that may asked about your interactions with your family and friends. I will do everything possible to minimize any discomfort you have concerning the questions asked during the interview. There may be uncommon or previously unknown risks. You should report any problems to the researcher.

How will your privacy be protected?

If you decide to participate in this study please understand that your participation is voluntary and that you have the right to withdraw your consent or discontinue participation at any time. You have the right to refuse to answer questions for any reason. In addition you individual privacy will be maintained in all published and written data resulting from the study. Participants' names will be replaced with pseudonyms in any and all write-ups. Taped interviews will be the property of the researcher, secured in a locked cabinet, and destroyed at the end of the project. Members of your school community may be aware that you are involved in a study regarding how students understand college.

Participants will not be identified in any report or publication about this study. Although every effort will be made to keep research records private, there may be times when federal or state law requires the disclosure of such records, including personal information. This is very unlikely, but if disclosure is ever required, University X will take steps allowable by law to protect the privacy of personal information. In some cases, your information in this research study could be reviewed by representatives of the University, research sponsors, or government agencies for purposes such as quality control or safety.

Will you receive anything for being in this study?

You will not receive anything for taking part in this study.

Will it cost you anything to be in this study?

There will be no costs for being in the study

What if you have questions about this study?

You have the right to ask, and have answered, any questions you may have about this research. If you have questions, or concerns, you should contact the researchers listed on the first page of this form.

What if you have questions about your rights as a research participant?

All research on human volunteers is reviewed by a committee that works to protect your rights and welfare. If you have questions or concerns about your rights as a research subject you may contact, anonymously if you wish, the Institutional Review Board at XXX-XXX-XXXX or by email to IRB_subjects@edu.

Participant's Agreement:

I have read the information provided above. I have asked all the questions I have at this time. I voluntarily agree to participate in this research study.

____

Signature of Research Participant   Date

____

Printed Name of Research Participant

____

Signature of Person Obtaining Consent   Date

____

Printed Name of Person Obtaining Consent

APPENDIX B: INTERVIEW PROTOCOL

Sample Interview Questions for Students

Sample Interview Questions for Fall of Senior Year:
- Can you tell me about your life in Mexico?
- Can you tell me about your schooling experiences in Mexico?
- Why did your family decide to come to the United States?
- How did your family come to the United States?
- Can you tell me about your schooling experiences in North Carolina?
- Is your life at home with your family different than your life at school?
- When did you know that you wanted to go to college?
- What are the main obstacles surrounding going to college?
- When did you realize that going to college might be more difficult for you than for other students?
- Why do you want to go to college?
- What are the steps you are taking to apply to college?
- What types of courses are you taking to prepare you for college?
- Does your family support and encourage you to pursue a college degree?
- Where do you get your information about college?
- Can you tell me what colleges you will apply to?
- What steps are you taking in high school to prepare you for college?
- What types of messages have you heard at BGHS about going to college?
- Do you know about the DREAM Act?
- If you had the chance to talk to congress why would you tell me that you should be able to go to college?

Sample Interview Questions for Spring of Senior Year:
- What courses are you taking in your final semester of school?
- Have you applied to college yet?
- Which colleges did you decide to apply to and why did you select those colleges?
- Have you spent time visiting the colleges you are applying to?
- Who is helping you apply to college?
- Do you understand your options where financial aid is concerned?

- What do you think will keep you from attending college?
- Could you and your family afford the cost of selective public university, approximately $30,000, for an out-of-state student, without any financial aid?
- Could you and your family afford the cost of the local community college, approximately $3000, for an out-of-state student, without any financial aid?
- Do you know other undocumented students who are applying to college?
- Did you have friends who already graduated who were undocumented? What did they do after high school?
- What will you do if you don't go to college?
- What would attending college mean to you? What will it mean for your future?

Sample Interview Questions for Teachers

Sample Interview Questions for Teachers:
- Can you tell me about your own background?
- Could you tell me about your role at the high school?
- Do you provide support for students to attend college? How?
- How does the Sunder Crossings community feel about Latino students attending college?
- How does the high school feel about Latino students attending college?
- Do you feel like the high school is a welcoming place for Latino students?
- Where do Latino students feel most comfortable at school?
- When did you usually learn that students are undocumented?
- What are your hopes and dreams for the undocumented students?
- Do you feel like the school helps prepare all students for life after high school?
- What do you know about undocumented students' opportunities to attend college?
- How much does family background influence students' college aspirations?
- How much does the high school community influence students' college aspirations?
- Which students do you feel have the best chance of attending college? Why?

- What types of barriers exist for the Latino students in the high school?
- What types of barriers exist during the college application for undocumented students?
- Why do you think students who are undocumented stay in high school?
- How do you feel about the admission policies for undocumented students in North Carolina?
- Do you think these policies are fair?
- Would you change the current policies? If so, how?
- How do you feel about working with undocumented students?
- How do you feel about working with recent immigrants?
- How do you think other teachers feel about working with undocumented students?
- How do you think other teachers feel about working with recent immigrants?
- How do you think the Sunder Crossings community feels about undocumented immigrants?
- What do you see undocumented students who have graduated from BGHS doing after high school?

APPENDIX C: ESTIMATE OF UNDOCUMENTED HIGH SCHOOL POPULATION IN NORTH CAROLINA

NC Department of Public Instruction

For the annual dropout rate calculation, a dropout is defined as a student who:

- was enrolled in school at some time during the previous school year, which is the reporting year;
- was not enrolled on Day 20 of the current school year;
- has not graduated from high school or completed a state or district approved educational program; and does not meet any of the following reporting exclusions:
  - transferred to another public school district, private school, home school or state/district approved educational program,
  - temporarily absent due to suspension or school-approved illness, or
  - death.

- **DPI Per Pupil Expenditures:** $6,741.39
- **DPI Total K-12 Latino student enrollment:** 88,355
- **DPI Total 9-12 Latino student enrollment:** 20,140
- **DPI Total Latino SENIORS:** 3057
- **DPI 2005 Projection of OVERALL Public High School Graduates:** 73,559
- **DPI Trend data on the percent of Hispanic students dropping out in grades 9-12:** 8.67%
- **DPI Latino student graduation rate:** 91%
- **DPI 2005 Projection of LATINO Public High School Graduates:** 2782
- **DPI High School Graduate Intentions:** NC public university (36%) and NCCCS (33%)

US Immigration and Naturalization Services Office of Policy and Planning

POPULATION PROJECTION

Most recent projections released in 2003 estimate that the total undocumented population in the United States is 7 million (17%). North Carolina, however, has an estimated undocumented population of 206,000 (44%).

- The US Dept. of Justice reported in 2003 that 68% of its prison population had not completed high school
- "Street gangs are an amalgam of racism, of urban underclass poverty, of minority and youth culture, of fatalism in the face of rampant deprivation, of political insensitivity, and the gross ignorance of inner city America on the part of us who don't have to survive there."
- Some studies out of Harvard University have linked school commitment and expectations of educational attainment can be linked to gang involvement.

Formula 1:

20,140   **x**   **.44**   **=**   **8862**
total # of Latino 9-12   INS % of NC undoc   total # of
undoc students
    students

Formula 2:

3057   **x**   **.44**   **=**   **1345**
total # of 2005 Latino   INS % of NC undoc   total # of
2005 undoc
    SENIORS   graduates

Formula 3:

1345   **x**   **.36**   **=**   **484**
total # of 2005 undoc   DPI proj% college   total # of
undoc students
    graduates   college bound

Formula 4:

1345   **x**   **.33**   **=**   **444**
total # of 2005 undoc   DPI proj% comcol   total # of
undoc students
    graduates   commcoll bound

Formula 5:

484   x   **$8,486**   =   **$4,107,224**
est of undoc coll   UNC per pupil cost   total appropriation
UNC

The information above provided in 2006 by the Marisol Jimenez-McGee, Advocacy Director and Lobbyist for El Pueblo Inc. located in Raleigh, North Carolina. For more information on El Pueblo please see their website at http://www.elpueblo.org/.

APPENDIX D: POSITIONALITY

"As personal experience researchers we owe our care, our responsibility, to the research participants and how our research texts shape their lives." (Clandenin & Connelly, 2000, p. 422) To meet that responsibility of a critical and reflexive ethnographer, I had to identify and evaluate my own positionality as a mixed-heritage researcher. Ethnography is never a neutral process but rather a political and moral process (Murillo, 1999). For this reason I embraced the label of Chicana ethnographer (Villenas, 1996) to stand in solidarity with my immigrant students, yet I recognize that this particular label may be too limiting as I grow and change, and as the context that I work in changes as well. I am a Chicana ethnographer but I also leave space for other descriptives to follow.

The academic world is anchored in a Eurocentric, "whitestream"(Grande, 2000) position. Because of my mixed heritage and light skin I have been able to walk in that world comfortably for most of my life. While I am mindful of my privilege, I can also use what I know to be a cultural broker for the undocumented students I worked with each day in the Latino Outreach program as well as in my research. Because of my white heritage and a background similar to their own (education, socioeconomic class, and skin color), I appear legitimate to those in power. I can state my position without appearing biased or trying to further my own cause. Because of my Latino heritage, I share the collective experiences of the Latino culture (family get-togethers, shared religious traditions, food) with my student participants. I understand enough Spanish that I could communicate with the students who were kind enough to put up with my bad grammar, and at the same time I was able to talk academic jargon and middle-class values with the white professionals and academics that I encountered.

My positionality is complex because I shared both commonalities and differences with the students that I worked with in my research. I also shared a life apart from my research as I served as the director of the mentoring/college prep program that worked with Latino immigrant students in Sunder Crossings, including some of those students in my research. As a researcher who believes in "situated knowledge" (Haraway, 1988), I believe that my work is only one vision of these undocumented students and that this vision came from the multiple points and multiple positions and roles that I played in each of their lives.

In my work as the director of the mentoring/college prep program, in which I was involved for three years, my identity and positionality was constantly renegotiated and reconstituted in different contexts. Differing contexts included being seen first as a stranger and then as a more familiar and comfortable figure after interaction with the students in the high school, in their community, and in the university setting. My identity and positionality also altered in response to working with students, their families, teachers, administrators and outside constituents. Throughout the research process I questioned who I was, and what role I could play in these students' lives, whether I emanated a sense of authentic caring (Valenzuela, 1999), and if I, too, wasn't setting these students up for failure in the higher education system.

By choosing to write an "ethnography of the particular" (Abu-Lughod, 1991), I incorporated my positionality along with the stories of the students' lives. My mixed-heritage allowed me to be both a guest and an outsider at the same time, and this allowed me to see from multiple viewpoints. As a mixed-heritage researcher I used my hybridity as a way to create mobile positioning that I hoped could improve the educational opportunities of the undocumented students I worked with, through, and for in the research. Positionality is the "story that writes my life," and I not only tried to be mindful of it as I thought about the process of reflexive ethnography and my influence on my research environment, but also used it in my work as an activist researcher.

References

Abu-Lughod, L. (1991). Writing against culture. In R. Fox (Ed.), *Recapturing anthropology: Working in the present* (pp. 137-162). Santa Fe, NM: School of American Research.

Adam, M. (2006). States are faking minority progress for no child left behind. *Education Digest Essential Readings Condensed for Quick Review, 71*(5), 18-23.

Albrecht, T. J. (2007). *Challenges and service needs of undocumented Mexican undergraduate students: Students' voices and administators' perspectives.* Doctoral dissertation at the University of Texas at Austin, 2007. Dissertation Abstracts International.

Aleinikoff, T., Martin, D., & Motomura, H. (2003). *Immigration and citizenship: Process and policy.* St. Paul, Minnesota: West Publishing.

Althusser, L. (1971). *Lenin and philosophy and other essays.* New York: Monthly Review Press.

Anderson, J. (1988). *The education of blacks in the south, 1860-1935.* Chapel Hill, NC: University of North Carolina Press.

Anzaldua, G. (1987). *Borderlands: The new mestiza = la frontera.* San Francisco: Spinster/Aunt Lute.

Auerbach, S. (2002). "Why do they give the good classes to some and not to others?" Latino parent narratives of struggle in a college access program. *Teachers College Record, 104*(7), 1369-1392.

Bailey, R. (2005). New immigrant communities in the North Carolina Piedmont Triad: Integration issues and challenges. In E. Gozdzia, & S. F. Martin (Eds.), *Beyond the gateway: Immigrants in a changing America.* (pp. 57-85). Lanham, MD: Lexington Books.

Barato, R. (2009). *Shadows in the classroom: undocumented Latino students in urban community colleges.* Doctoral dissertation, New York University, 2009.

Bell, D. (2005). In Delgado R., Stefancic J. (Eds.), *The Derrick Bell reader.* New York: New York University Press.

Bell, D. (1992). *Race, racism and American law* (3rd Edition). Boston: Little Brown.

Bell, D. (1985). The civil rights chronicles: The chronicle of the divine gift. *99 Harvard Law Review, 4.*

Bell, D. (1979). Bakke, minority admission, and the usual price of racial remedies. *California Law Review, 67*(1), 3-19.

Bettie, J. (2003). *Women without class: Girls, race, and identity.* Berkeley: University of California Press.

Bhatkin, M. M. (1986). In Emerson, C. & Holquist, M. (Eds.), *Speech genres and other late essays.* Austin: University of Texas Press.

Bourdieu, P. (1998). *Acts of resistance: Against the tyranny of the market.* New York: The New York Press.

Bourdieu, P. (1986). The forms of capital. In J. G. Richardson (Ed.). *Handbook of theory and research* (pp. 241-258). New York: Greenwood Press.

Bowles, H., & Gintis, S. (1976). At the root of the problem: The capitalist economy. In S. Bowles, & H. Gintis (Eds.), *Schooling in capitalist America: Educational reform and contradictions in economic life* (pp. 53-101). New York: Basic Books Inc.

Brayboy, B. (2004). Hiding in the ivy: American Indian students and visibility in elite educational settings. *Harvard Educational Review, 74*(2), 125-152.

Brimelow, P. (1995). *Alien nation: Common sense about America's immigration disaster.* New York: Random House.

Carreon, G., Drake, C., & Barton, A. (2005). The importance of presence: Immigrant parents' school engagement experiences. *American Educational Research Journal, 42*(3), 465-498.

Carter, P. (2005). *Keepin it real': School success beyond black and white.* New York: Oxford University Press.

Center for Immigration Studies(2006). Quote for first foot note retrieved on October 25, 2006 at http://www.cis.org/articles/2006/mskoped032406.html.

Clandenin, J., & Connelly, M. (2000). *Narrative inquiry: Experience and story in qualitative research.* San Francisco: Jossey-Bass Publishers.

Conchas, G. & Clark, P. (2002). Career academies and urban minority schooling: Forging optimism despite limited opportunity. *Journal of Education for Students Placed at Risk.* 7 (3), 287-311.

Cortes, R. D. (2008). *"Cursed and blessed.": Examining the socioemotional and academic experiences of undocumented Latina/o community college students.* Doctoral dissertation, Claremont Graduate University, 2008. Dissertation Abstracts International

Clandinin, J., & Connelly, M. (2003). Personal experience methods. In J. W. Creswell (Ed.), *Research design: Qualitative, quantitative, and mixed methods approaches.* Thousand Oaks, CA: Sage Publications.

Conchas, G. (2006). *The color of success: Race and high-achieving urban youth.* New York: Teachers College Press.

Cornelius, W. (2004). Ambivalent reception: Mass public responses to the "new" Latino immigration to the United States. In M. Suárez-Orozco, & M. Paez (Eds.), *Latinos remaking America.* Berkeley: University of California Press.

Cortina, R., & Gendreau, M. (Eds.). (2003). *Immigrants and schooling: Mexicans in New York.* New York: Center for Migration Studies.

Crenshaw, K. (1993). Mapping the margins: Intersectionality, identity politics and the violence against women of color. *Stanford Law Review, 43,* 1241-1299.

Crenshaw, K., Gotanda, N., Peller, G., & Thomas, K. (Eds.) (1995). *Critical race theory: The key writings that formed the movement.* New York: The New Press.

Cummins, J. (1995). Power and pedagogy in the education of culturally-diverse students. In J. Frederickson (Ed.), *Reclaiming our voices: Bilingual education, critical pedagogy, and praxis* (pp. 139-162). Los Angeles: California Association for Bilingual Education.

Cummins, J. (1986). Empowering minority students: A framework for achievement. *Harvard Educational Review, 56,* 18-36.

Cummins, J. (1980). The cross-lingual dimensions of language proficiency: Implications for bilingual education and optimal age issue. *TESOL Quarterly, 14*(2), 175-187.

Davies, C. (1999). *Reflexive ethnography: A guide to researching selves and others.* New York: Routledge.

Kirsten Day, Et Al. v. Kathleen Sebelius, Governor of Kansas, July (Case 5:04-cv-o485-RDR-JPO 2005).

de Certau, M. (1984). *The practice of everyday life.* Berkeley: University of California Press.

De Leon, Sylvia Adelle. (2005). *Assimilation and ambiguous experience of the resilient male Mexican immigrants that successfully navigate American higher education.* University of Texas-Austin Doctoral Dissertation.

Delgado, R. (1995). *Critical race theory: The cutting edge.* Philadelphia: Temple University Press.

Delgado, R., & Stefancic, J. (1998). *The Latino condition: A critical reader.* New York: New York University Press.

Delgado, R., & Stefancic, J. (1989). Why do we all tell the same stories?: Law reform, critical librarianship, and the triple helix dilemma. *Stanford Law Review, 42*(1), 207-225.

Delgado, R., & Stefanic, J. (Eds.). (2001). *Critical race theory: An introduction.* New York: New York University Press.

Delgado-Bernal, D. (2002). Critical race theory, Latino critical theory and critical race-gendered epistemologies: Recognizing students of color as holders and creators of knowledge. *Qualitative Inquiry, 8*(1), 105-123.

Delgado-Bernal, D. (1998). Using a Chicana feminist epistemology in educational research. *Harvard Educational Review, 68*(1), 555-581.

Delgado-Gaitan, C. (1992). School matters in the Mexican-American home: Socializing children to education. *American Educational Research Journal, 29*(3), 495-513.

Dewalt, K., & Dewalt, B. (2002). *Participant observation: A guide for fieldworkers.* New York: Altamira Press.

Donato, R. (1997). *The other struggle for equal schools: Mexican Americans during the civil rights era.* New York: SUNY Press.

Donato, R. (1996). The irony of year-round schools: Mexican migrant resistance in a California community during the civil rights era *Educational Administration Quarterly, 32*(2), 181-208.

Dozier, S. B. (2001). Undocumented and documented international students: A comparative study of their academic performance. *Community College Review, 2*, 43-53.

Dozier, S. B. (1995). Undocumented immigrant students at an urban community college: A demographic and academic profile. *Migration World, 23*(1-2), 20-22.

Dozier, S. B. (1992). Emotional concerns for undocumented and out of status foreign students. *Community Review, 13*(1-2), 33-38.

DuBois, W. E. (1993). Double-consciousness and the veil. In C. Lemert (Ed.), *Social theory: The multicultural and classic readings.* Boulder: Westview Press.

El Pueblo Inc. (2005). *Undocumented information: Interview with Marisol Jimenez.* Raleigh, NC: El Pueblo Inc.

Erisman, W. & Looney, S. (April, 2007). *Opening the door to the American dream: Increasing the higher education and success for immigrants.* Washington, D.C. Institute for Higher Education Policy. Retrieved on August 1, 2009 at http://www.ihep.org/Publications/publications-detail.cfm?id=55

Emerson, R., Fritz, R., & Shaw, L. (1995). *Writing ethnographic fieldnotes.* Chicago: University of Chicago Press.

Fergus, E. (2002). Everyone sees my skin color differently: Phenotype and ethnic identifications in the perception of opportunity and academic orientation of

Mexican and Puerto Rican youth. *University of Michigan Doctoral Dissertation.*

Fernandez, L. (2002). Telling stories about school: Using critical race and Latino critical theories to document Latina/Latino education and resistance. *Qualitative Inquiry, 8*(1), 45-65.

Fernandez-Kelly, P. M., & Schauffler, R. (1994). Divided fates: Immigrant children in a restructured U.S. economy. *International Migration Review, 28*(4), 662.

Fine, M. (1990). *Framing dropouts: Notes on the politics of an urban high school.* Albany, NY: State University of New York Press.

Flores, S. (forthcoming 2010). State "dream acts": The effect of in-state resident tuition policies on college enrollment of undocumented Latino students in the United States. *The Review of Higher Education.*

Flores, S. (2006). *The effect of in-state resident tuition eligibility on the college enrollment of undocumented Latino students in Texas.* Paper presented at the 31st Annual Association for the Study of Higher Education Annual Conference (November 2-4, 2006, Anaheim, CA).

Flores, S. & Chapa, J. (2009). Latino immigrant access to higher education in a bipolar contexst of reception. *Journal of Hispanic Higher Education,* 8 (1), pp.80-109.

Flores, S. & Horn, C. (2009). College persistence among undocumented students at a selective public university: A quantitative case study analysis. *Journal of College Student Retention, 11, 57-76.*

Flores, S. & Osoguera, L. (2009). The community college and undocumented immigrant students across state contexts: localism and public policy. In. R. Crowson & E. Goldring (Eds.), *the new localism in American Education* (pp.63-85). National Society for the Study of Education, Vol. 1. New York: Teachers College.

Focault, M. (1991). Governmentality. In G. Burchell, C. Gordon & P. Miller (Eds.), *The Focault effect: Studies in governmentality.* Chicago: The University of Chicago Press.

Focault, M. (1980). Truth and power. In C. Gordon (Ed.), *Power/Knowledge: Selected interviews and other writings 1972-1977.* New York: Pantheon Books.

Foner, N. (2000). *From Ellis island to JFK: New York's two great waves of immigration.* New Haven, CT: Yale University Press.

Freire, P. (1970). *Pedagogy of the oppressed.* New York: Continuum International Publishing.

Fry, R. (2002). *Latinos in higher education: Many to enroll, few to graduate.* Washington, D.C.: Pew Hispanic Center.

Fry, R. (2004). *Latino youth finishing college: The role of selective pathways.* Washington, D.C.: Pew Hispanic Center.

Gandara, P. (2006). *Fragile futures: Risk and vulnerability among Latino high achievers*. Princeton, NJ: Educational Testing Services.

Gandara, P. (1995). *Over the ivy walls: The educational mobility of low-income Chicanos*. New York: SUNY series, social context of education.

Garcia, E. (2001). *Hispanic in the United States education: Raices y alas*. Lanham, MD: Rowman & Littlefield Publishers.

Geertz, C. (1973). *The interpretation of cultures*. New York: Basic Books.

Gibson, M., Gandara, P., & Koyama, J. (2004). *School connections: U.S. Mexican youth, peers, and school achievement*. New York: Teachers College Press.

Gibson, M. (1988). *Accommodation without assimilation: Sikh immigrants in an American high school*. Ithaca, NY: Cornell University Press.

Glesne, C. (1999). *Becoming qualitative researchers: An introduction* (2nd ed.). New York: Longman.

Godson, I. (2005, House bill proposes in-state tuition for illegal immigrants. *The Technician*.

Goldring, L. (1998) The power of status in transnational social fields. In M. P. Smith & L. E. Guarnizo (Eds.), *Transnationalism from below* (pp. 165-195). New Brunswick, NJ: Transaction Publishers.

Gonzales, R. (2009). *Young lives on hold: The college dreams of undocumented students*. The College Board. Retrieved on Setpember 30th, 2009 at http://professionals.collegeboard.com/profdownload/young-lives-on-hold-college-board.pdf.

Gonzalez, G. (1990). *Chicano education in the era of segregation*. Philadelphia: Balch Institute Press.

Gonzalez, K., Stoner, C., & Jovel, J. (2003). Examining the role of social capital in access to college for Latinas: Toward a college opportunity framework. *Journal of Hispanic Higher Education, 2*(1), 146-170.

Gonzalez, N., Moll, L., & Amanti, C. (2005). *Funds of knowledge: Theorizing practices in households, communities and classrooms*. New Jersey: Lawrence Erlbaum.

Goodall, H. L. (2000). *Writing the new ethnography*. Lanham, Maryland: Rowman & Littlefield Publishers.

Grande, S. (2000). American Indian geographies of identity and power: At the crossroads of *indigena* and *mestizaje*. *Harvard Educational Review, 70*(4), 467-498.

Hamann, E. T., Zúñiga, V., & Sánchez García, J. (2006). Pensando en cynthia y su hermana: Educational implications of United States-Mexico transnationalism for children. *Journal of Latinos and Education, 5*(4), 253-274.

Haney Lopez, I. (1996). *White by law: The legal construction of race*. New York: New York University Press.

Haraway, D. (1988). Situated knowledges: The science question in feminism and the privilege of partial perspective. *Feminist Studies, 14*(3), 575-599.

Harris, C. (1993). Whiteness as property. Harvard Law Review 106.

Hill Collins, P.(1999). *Black feminist thought: Knowledge, consciousness, and the politics of empowerment.* New York: Routledge Publishing.

Holland, D., Lachicotte, W., Skinner, D., & Cain, C. (1998). *Identity and agency in cultural worlds.* Cambridge, MA: Harvard University Press.

Holland, D., & Lave, J. (2000). *History in person: Enduring struggles, contentious practice, intimate identities.* Santa Fe, NM: School of American Research Press.

Horvat, E., Weininger, E., & Lareau, A. (2003). From social ties to social capital: Class differences in the relations between schools and parent networks. *Parent Networks, 40*(2), 319-351.

Huntington, S. P. (2004). *The Hispanic Challenge.* Retrieved on October 15, 2006 at www.foreignpolicy.com.

Jimenez, M., Zarate, M., & Wiggins, M. (2005). A lot of dreams are being crushed: The legislature's failure to offer in-state tuition to undocumented students will cost North Carolina much more than the money it saved. *The Independent Weekly.* Retrieved on January 5, 2007 at http://www.indyweek.com/gyrobase/Content?oid=oid%3A25015.

Johnson, K. (2000). Race matters: Immigration law and policy scholarship, law in the ivory tower, and the legal indifference of the race critique. *Illinois Law Review* Summer 2000.

Johnson, K. (1997). Some thoughts on the future of Latino legal scholarship. *Harvard Latino Law Review, 2,* 101-144.

Jordan, M. (2006). Illegal at Princeton. *Wall Street Journal.* Retrieved on January 20, 2007 at http://users1.wsj.com/lmda/do/checkLogin?mg=wsj-users1&url=http%3A%2F%2Fonline.wsj.com%2Farticle%2FSB11450593 7960426590.html%3Femailf%3Dyes.

Kandel, W., & Parrado, E. (2004). Hispanics in the American South and the transformation of the poultry industry. In D. Arreola (Ed.), *Hispanic spaces, Latino spaces: Community and cultural diversity in contemporary America.* Austin: University of Texas Press.

Kasarda, J., & Johnson, J. (2006). *The economic impact of the Hispanic population on the state of North Carolina.* University North Carolina at Chapel Hill: Kenan-Flagler Business School.

Kirsanow, P. (May 10, 2006). Illegal advantage: Lawbreakers vault to the front of the college-admissions line. *The National Review Online.* Retrieved on January 24, 2007 at http://article.nationalreview.com/?q=OTUyNzg5YWFiZDU5NjU4 ZjY0ZTUyMDMwZWM4NTQ5YzY=.

Kohler, A., & Lazarin, M. (2007). *Hispanic education in the United States: Statistical brief No. 8.* Washington, D.C: National Council of La Raza.

Krissman, F. (2000). Immigrant labor recruitment: U.S. agribusiness and undocumented migration from Mexico. In N. Foner, R. Rumbaut, & S. Gold (Eds.), *Immigration research for a new century* (pp. 277-300). New York: Russell Sage.

Kruger, C. (2006). *In-state tuition for undocumented immigrants*. ECS State Notes. Denver, CO: Education Commission of the States.

Ladson-Billings, G., & Tate, William F. (1995). Toward a critical race theory of education. *Teachers College Record, 1*, 47-68.

Lareau, A. (2000). *Home advantage*. Lanham, MD: Rowman & Littlefield.

Lee, J.B., Frishberg, E., Shkodriani, G.M., Freeman, S.A., Magnnis, A.M. & Bob, S.H. (2009). *Study on the admission of undocumented students into the North Carolina community college system*. A report to the North Carolina Community College System. Bethesda, MD. JBL Associates, Inc.

Lopez, J. (2004). *"The right stuff": Attitudes of high-achieving Latino youth toward higher education*. Boulder, CO: University of Colorado.

Lorde, A. (1992). Age, race, class and sex: Women redefining difference. In M. Anderson, & P. Hill Collins (Eds.) *Race, class and gender: An anthology* (495-502). Belmont, CA: Wadsworth.

Marabel, M. (1992). *Black America*. Westfield, NJ: Open Media.

Massey, D., Durand, J., & Malone, N. J. (2002). *Beyond smoke and mirrors: Mexican immigration in an era of economic integration*. New York: Russell Sage Foundation.

Matsuda, M. (1993). *Words that wound: Critical race theory, assaultive speech and the first amendment*. Boulder, CO: Westview Press.

McIntosh, P. (1988). White privilege: Unpacking the invisible knapsack. In B. Schneider (Ed.), *An anthology: Race in the first person* (pp. 119-126). New York: Crown Trade Paperbacks.

McLaren, P. (1993). *Schooling as a ritual performance: Towards a political economy of education symbols and gestures* (2nd ed.). New York: Routledge.

Mehan, H. (1994). *Tracking untracking: The consequences of placing low track students in high track classes*. Santa Cruz: National Center for Research on Cultural Diversity and Second Language Learning.

Moll, L., Amanti, C., Neff, D., & Gonzalez, D. (1992). Funds of knowledge for teaching: Using a qualitative approach to connect homes and classrooms. *Theory into Practice, 31*(2), 132-141.

Moll, L., & Ruiz, R. (2002). The schooling of Latino children. In M. Suárez-Orozco, & M. Paez (Eds.), *Latinos: Remaking America* (pp. 362-388). Berkeley: University of California Press.

Moltz, D. (2009). 'Hollow victory for undocumented students'. *In Inside Higher Ed*. Retrieved on September 21, 2009 at http://www.insidehighered.com/news/2009/09/21/immigrants

Motomura, H. (2006). *Americans in waiting: The lost story of immigration and citizenship in the United States.* Oxford: Oxford University Press.

Murdock, S. (2006). *Population change in the United States: Implications for human and socioeconomic resources in the 21st century.* San Antonio, TX: Institute for Demographic and Socioeconomic Research, University of Texas-San Antonio.

Murillo, E. (2002). How does it feel to be a problem? In S. Stanton Wortham, Murillo, Jr., Enrique G & E. T. Hamann (Eds.), *Education in the new Latino diaspora : Policy and the politics of identity.* Westport, Conneticut: Ablex Publishing.

Murillo, E. (1999). Mojado crossings along neoliberal borderlands. *Educational Foundations, 13*(1), 7-30.

National Conference on State Legislatures. (2005). *College tuition and undocumented immigrants report.* Denver, CO: National Conference of State Legislatures.

National Immigration Law Center. (2005, February). *The economic benefits of the DREAM act and the student adjustment act.* Retrieved on November 3, 2007 at http://www.nilc.org/immlawpolicy/DREAM/Econ_Bens_DREAM&Stdnt_ Adjst_0205.pdf.

National Immigration Law Center. (2006). *DREAM act: Basic information.* Retrieved June 5, 2006, 2006 at http://www.nilc.org/immlawpolicy/DREAM/dream_basic_info_0406.pdf.

National Immigration Law Center (2009, February). Basic facts about in-state tuition for undocumented immigrant students. Retrieved on September 5, 2009 from http://www.nilc.org/immlawpolicy/dream/instate-tuition-basicfacts-2009-02-23.pdf

Nevins, J. (2002). *Operation gatekeeper: The rise of "illegal alien" and the making of the U.S. Mexico boundary.* New York: Rutledge Publishing.

Ngai, M.(2004). *Impossible subjects: Illegal aliens and the making of modern America.* New Jersey: Princeton University Press.

Noblit, G., Murillo, E. G., Jr., & Flores, S. (2004). *Postcritical ethnography: Reinscribing critique.* Creskill, NJ: Hampton Press.

North Carolina Society of Hispanic Professionals (2005). Community colleges in North Carolina accepting undocumented immigrants. Retrieved on October 2, 2005 at http://www.thencshp.org/New%20Folder/UDI%20Acceptance%20Chart% 20NC%20Community%20Colleges.pdf.

North Carolina Society of Hispanic Professionals (2004). Guidelines on the admissions of undocumented aliens. Retrieved on October 2, 2005 at http://www.thencshp.org/New%20Folder/Guidelines%20%20Admission% 20to%20UNC%20System.pdf.

North Carolina Society of Hispanic Professionals (2004). Update on access to higher education for Hispanic/Latino students from the federal to local level. Retrieved on October 2, 2005 at http://www.thencshp.org/New%20Folder/ Access%20 to% 20 Higher%20Education.pdf.

Olivas, M. (2009). Undocumented college student, taxation and financial aid: A technical note. *Review of Higher Education, 32* (3), pp. 407-416.

Olivas, M. (2008, July/August). Colleges and undocumented students. *Change,* pp. 20-21.

Olivas, M. (2005). The story of PLYLER v DOE: The education of undocumented children, and the polity In D. Martin, & P. Schuck (Eds.), *Immigration stories* (pp. 197-220). New York: Foundation Press.

Olivas, M. (2004). IRIRA, the DREAM act and undocumented college student residency. *30 J.C.U.L. 435,* (435-464).

Olivas, M. (June, 2002). A rebuttal to fair. *University Business, 72.*

Olivas, M. (1995). Storytelling out of school: Undocumented college residency, race and reaction. *Hastings Constitutional Law Quarterly, 22,* 1019-1086.

Olivas, M. (1994). Preempting preemption: Foreign affairs, state rights and alien classifications. *35 Virginia Journal of International Law 217.*

Olivas, M. (1990). The chronicles, my grandfather's stories, and immigration law: The slave traders chronicle as racial history. *St. Louis University Law Journal 425.*

Olivas, M. (1988). Administering intentions: Law, theory, practice and postsecondary requirements. *Journal of Higher Education, 59*(3), 263-286.

Oliverez, P. (2005). *High aspirations, tough choices: How ineligibility for financial aid shapes college choice for college-ready undocumented immigrant students.* Paper presented at the 30th Annual Association for the Study of Higher Education Annual Conference (November 17-19, 2005, Philadelphia, PA).

Oliverez, P. (2005). *Ready and (un)able: An ethnographic study of the challenges of college access and financial aid for undocumented students in the united states.* University of Southern California Doctoral Dissertation.

Oliverez, P., Chavez, M., Soriano, M., & Tierney, W. (2006). *The college & financial aid guide for AB 540 undocumented immigrant students.* Los Angeles, CA: Center for Higher Education Policy Analysis, The University of Southern California.

Orfield, G., Losen, D., Wald, J., Swanson, CB. (2004). *Losing our future: How minority youth are being left behind by the graduation rate crisis.* Boston: Harvard Education Publishing Group.

Olsen, L. (1997). *Made in America: Immigrant students in our public schools.* New York: The New Press.

Parker, L., & Lynn, M. (2002). What's race got to do with it? Critical race theory's conflicts with and connections to qualitative research methodology and epistemology. *Qualitative Inquiry, 8*(1), 7-22.

Parker, L., Deyhle, D., & Villenas, S.(Eds.) (1999). *Race is...race isn't: Critical race theory and qualitative studies in education*. Boulder, CO: Westview Press.

Parrado, E and Valencia, J (forthcoming 2010). "How high is Hispanic/Mexican fertility in the U.S.? Immigration and tempo consideration." Presented at the Annual Meeting of the Population Association of America. (April 15-17, 2010, Dallas, TX)

Passel, J.S. & Cohen, D. (2008). *Trends in unauthorized immigration: undocumented inflow now tails legal inflow*. Retrieved on August 1, 2008 at http://pewhispanic.org/reports/report.php?ReportID=94

Passel, J. S., & Fix, M. (2004). *Undocumented immigrants: Facts and figures*. Washington D.C.: The Urban Institute.

Perez, W. (2006). *Loss of talent: Highly gifted undocumented students in the United States*. Paper presented at the 31st Annual Association for the Study of Higher Education Annual Conference (November 2-4, 2006, Anaheim, CA).

Perez, W., Espinoza, R., Coronade, H.M., Cortes, R. & Ramos, K. (2009). Academic resilience among undocumented Latino students. *Hispanic Journal of Behavioral Science*, 31 (2), pp. 149-181.

Perna, L. (2000). Differences in the decision to attend college among African American, Hispanics and Whites. *The Journal of Higher Education, 71*(2), 117-134.

Perna, L., & Titus, M. (2005). The relationship between parental involvement as social capital and college enrollment: An examination of racial/ethnic group differences. *The Journal of Higher Education, 76*(5), 485-517.

Perry, A. (2006). Toward a theoretical framework for membership: The case of undocumented immigrants and financial aid for postsecondary education *Review of Higher Education, 30*(1), 21-41.

Peshkin, A. (1988). In search of subjectivity: One's own. *Educational Researcher, 17*(7), 17-22.

Pew Hispanic Center (2006). Estimates of the unauthorized migrant population for states based on the March 2005 CPS. Retreived on January 5, 2007 at http://pewhispanic.org/factsheets/factsheet.php?FactsheetID=17. Washington, DC: Pew Hispanic Center.

Pickus, N. (2006). *Truth, faith and allegiance: Immigration and American civic nationalism*. Princeton, NJ: Princeton University Press.

Plyer v. Doe (1982). 457 U.S. 202 No. 80-1538.

Portes, A. (2004). The new Latin nation: Immigration and the Hispanic population in the United States. *Center for Migration and Development: Working Paper Series, Working Paper #04-02*.

Portes, A., & Rumbaut, R. (2001). *Legacies: The story of the immigrant second generation*. Berkeley: University of California Press.

Protopsaltis, S. (2005). *Undocumented immigrant students and access to higher education: An overview of federal and state policy.* Denver, CO: Bell Policy Report Center.

Reese, W. (1995). *The origins of the American high school.* Binghamton, New York: Vail-Ballou Press.

Reimers, D. (1998). *Unwelcome strangers: American identity and the turn against immigration.* New York: Columbia University Press.

Reissman, C. (1993). *Narrative analysis.* Newbury Park, California: Sage Publications.

Rincon, A. (2008). *Undocumented immigrants and higher education.* New York: LFB Scholarly.

Rivera, A. (1997). *Cybraceros.* Los Angeles, CA: Alex Rivera Productions.

Report to the Illinois General Assembly on House Resolution No. 892. (2002). *Changing demographics changing educational needs.* Retrieved on September 15, 2006 at http://209.85.165.104/search?q=cache:OdBBjhRZT-8J:www.ibhe.org/ Board/Agendas/2002/December/Item%25208Report.pdf+Report+to+the+Il linois+General+Assembly+on+House+Resolution+No.+892&hl=en&ct=cl nk&cd=2&gl=us

San Miguel, G. (1987). *Let them all take heed: Mexican Americans and the campaign for educational equality in Texas 1910-1981.* Austin: University of Texas Press.

Sanchez, P. (2001). Adopting transnationalism theory and discourse: Making space for a transnational Chicana. *Discourse: Studies in the Cultural Politics of Education, 22*(3), 374-381.

Sanjek, R. (1990). *Fieldnotes: The making of anthropology.* Ithaca, NY: Cornell University Press.

Santiago, D. (2004). *Federal policy and Latinos in higher education.* Washington, D.C.: Pew Hispanic Center.

Scott, J. (1990). *Domination and the arts of resistance: Hidden transcripts.* Yale University Press: New Haven.

Singer, A. (2004). *The rise of new immigrant gateways.* Washington, DC: Center on Urban and Metropolitan Policy, The Brookings Institution.

Solis, J. (2005). Transborder violence and undocumented youth: Extending cultural-historical analysis in transnational immigration studies. In Z. C. Daiute, C. Beykong, D. Higson-Smith & L. Nucci (Eds.), *International perspectives on youth conflict and development* (pp. 305-319). New York: Oxford University Press.

Solis, J. (2004). Narrating and counternarrating illegality as an identity. In C. C. Dauite, & C. Lightfoot (Eds.), *Narrative analysis: Studying the development of individuals in society* (pp. 181-199). New York: Sage Publications.

Solis, J. (2003). Re-thinking illegality as violence against, not by undocumented immigrants, children, and youth. *Journal of Social Issues, 59*(1), 15-31.

Solis, J. (2001). Immigration status and identity: Undocumented Mexicans in new York. In A. Lao-Montes, & A. Davila (Eds.), *Mambo montage: The Latinization of New York*. New York: Columbia University Press.

Solórzano, D., Villapando, O., & Oseguera, L. (2005). Educational inequities and Latina/o undergraduate students in the United States: A critical race analysis of their educational progress. *Journal of Hispanic Higher Education, 4*(3), 272-304.

Solórzano, D., & Delgado-Bernal, D. (2001). Examining transformational resistance through a critical race and LatCrit theory framework: Chicana and Chicano students in an urban context. *Urban Education, 36*(3), 308-342.

Solórzano, D., & Yosso, T. (2002). Critical race methodology: Counter-storytelling as an analytical framework for education research. *Qualitative Inquiry, 8*(1), 23-44.

Solórzano, D., & Yosso, T. (2002). A critical race theory counterstory of affirmative action in higher education. *Equity and Excellence in Education, 35*(2), 155-168.

Solórzano, D., & Yosso, T. (2001). Critical race and LatCrit theory and method: Counter-storytelling: Chicana and Chicano graduate school experiences. *Qualitative Studies in Education, 14*(4), 471-495.

Smith, M. P. & Guarnizo, L. E. (1998). The locations of transnationalism. In M. P. Smith & L. E. Guarnizo (Eds.), *Transnationalism from below* (pp. 3-34). New Brunswick, NJ: Transaction Publishers.

Spradley, J. (1980). *Participant observation*. Fort Worth: Harcourt Brace Jovanovich.

Stancill, J. (2005). Taking sides on tuition. *The Raleigh News and Observer*. Retrieved on November 4, 2005 at http://www.newsandobserver.com.libproxy.lib.unc.edu/news/q/archive/story/2342610p-870339c.html

Stake, R. (1995). *The art of case study research*. Thousand Oaks, CA: Sage Publications.

Stanton, W., Murillo, E. G.,Jr, Hamann, E. T., & (Eds). (2001). *Education in the new Latino diaspora: Policy and the politics of identity*. Westpost, CT: Ablex Publishing.

Stanton-Salazar, R. (1995). Social capital in the reproduction of inequality: Information networks among Mexican-origin high school students. *Sociology of Education, 68*, 116-135.

Stanton-Salazar, R., & Spina, S. (2003). Informal mentors and role models in the lives of urban Mexican-origin adolescents. *Anthropology and Education Quarterly, 34*(3), 231-254.

Stanton-Salazar, R., & Spina, S. (2000). The network orientation of highly resilient urban minority youth: A network-analytic account of minority socialization and its educational implications. *Urban Review, 32*(3), 227-261.

Stanton-Salazar, R. D. (2001). *Manufacturing hope and despair: The school and kin support networks of U.S.-Mexican youth.* New York: Sociology of education Series.

Stanton-Salazar, R. D. (1997). A social capital framework for understanding the socialization of racial minority children and youths. *Harvard Educational Review, 67*(1), 1-40.

Stanton-Salazar, R. D., & Dornbusch, S. M. (1995). Social capital and the reproduction of inequality: Information networks among Mexican-origin high school students. *Sociology of Education*, 68 (2), 116-35.

Stanton-Salazar, R. D., & Spina, S. U. (2000). The network orientations of highly resilient urban minority youth: A network-analytic account of minority socialization and its educational implications. *Urban Review, 32*(3), 227-261.

Suárez-Orozco, C., & Suárez-Orozco, M. (2001). *Children of immigration.* Cambridge, MA: Harvard University Press.

Suárez-Orozco, M. (1989). *Central American refugees and U.S. high schools.* Stanford, CA: Stanford University Press.

Suárez-Orozco, M. (1989). Psychosocial aspects of achievement motivation among recent Hispanic immigrants? In H. T. Trueba, G. Spindler & L. Spindler (Eds.), *What do anthropologists say about dropouts?*. New York: The Falmer Press.

Suárez-Orozco, M., & Paez, M. (2002). *Latinos remaking America.* Berkeley: University of California Press.

Suárez-Orozco, M., Suárez-Orozco, C., & Qin-Hilliard, D.(2001). *Interdisciplinary perspectives on the new immigration .* New York: Routledge.

Tate, W. F. (1997). Critical race theory and education: History, theory, and implications. *Review of Research in Education, 22*, 195-247.

The National Center for Public Policy and Higher Education. (2004). *The educational pipeline: Big investments, big returns.* Washington, D.C.: The National Center for Public Policy and Higher Education.

Tolbert, C., & Hero, R. (1996). Race/ethnicity and direct democracy: An analysis of California's illegal immigration initiative. *The Journal of Politics, 58*(3), 806-818.

Tomas Rivera Policy Institute. (2005). *The new Latino south and the challenge to the public education.* Los Angeles, CA: Tomas Rivera Policy Institute.

Trueba, E. (2004). *The new Americans: Immigrants and transnationals at work.* Lanham, Maryland: Roman & Little Publishers.

Trueba, E. (2002). Multiple ethnic, racial, and cultural identities in action: From marginality to a new cultural capital in modern society. *Journal of Latinos in Education, 1*(1), 7-28.

Trueba, E., & Bartolome, L.(2000). *Immigrant voices: In search of educational equity*. Lanham, MD: Rowman & Littlefield Publishers.

Tyack, D. (1974). *The one best system: A history of American urban education* . Boston: Harvard University Press.

U.S. Census. (2004). *American community survey*.

United States General Accounting Office. (2004). *Illegal alien school children: Issues in estimating state by state costs*. Washington DC: U.S. General Accounting Office.

University of North Carolina Tomorrow Commission (2007, December). University of North Carolina Tomorrow Commision Final Report. Retrieved on September 15, 2009 at http://www.northcarolina.edu/nctomorrow/index.htm

Urrieta, L. (2009) *Working from Within: Chicana and Chicano ActivistEducators in Whitestream Schools*. Tucson; University of Arizona Press.

Urrieta, L. (2007). Identity production in figured worlds: How Mexican Americans become Chicana/o activist educators. Paper presented at the University of North Carolina-Chapel Hill School of Education (March 8, 2007).

Urrieta, L. (2005). "Playing the game" versus "selling out": Chicanas and Chicanos relationship to whitestream schools. In B. K. Alexander, G. L. Anderson & B. P. Gallegos (Eds.), *Performance theories in education: Power, pedagogy, and the politics of identity* (pp. 173-196). Mahwah, MJ: Lawrence Erlbaum and Associates.

Urrieta, L. (2003). Orchestrating the selves: Chicana and Chicano negotiations of identity, ideology, and activism in education. *University of North Carolina Doctoral Dissertation.*

Urrieta, L., Gonzalez, M. S., Plata, O., Garcia, E., & Torres, M. (2003). Testimonios de inmigrantes: Students educating future teachers. *Journal of Latinos and Education, 2*(4), 233-243.

Valdes, F. (1996). Forward: Latina/o ethnicities, critical race theory, and post-identity politics in postmodern legal culture: From practices to possibilities. *La Raza Law Journal, 9*, 1-31.

Valdes, F. (1996). LatCrit theory: Naming and launching a new direction of critical legal scholarship. *Harvard Latino Law Review, 2*(1-59).

Valdes, F. (1998). Race, ethnicity, and nationhood: Forward: Under construction-LatCrit consciousness, community and theory. *La Raza Law Journal 1089.*

Valdes, F. (1997). Poised at the cusp: LatCrit theory, outsider jurisprudence and Latina/o self-empowerment. *Harvard Latino Law Review 101.*

Valdes, G. (1998). The world outside and inside schools: Language and immigrant children. *Educational Researcher, 27*(6), 4-18.

Valdes, G. (1996). *Con respeto: Bridging the distance between culturally diverse families and schools: An ethnographic portrait*. New York: Teachers College Press.

Valencia, E., & Johnson, V. (2006). Latino students in North Carolina: Acculturation, perceptions of school environeel, and academic aspirations. *Hispanic Journal of Behavioral Sciences, 28*(3), 350-367.

Valenzuela, A., & Foley, D. (2002). Critical ethnography: The politics of collaboration. In N. Denzin, & Y. Lincoln (Eds.), *The SAGE handbook of qualitative research* (217-235). Thousand Oaks, California: Sage Publications Inc.

Valenzuela, A. (1999). *Subtractive schooling: U.S.-Mexican youth and the politics of caring.* New York: SUNY series, the social context of education.

Vasquez, M., Seales, C., & Marquadt, M. (2007). New Latino destinations. In H. Rodriguez, R. Saenz & C. Menjivar (Eds.), *Latino/a sourcebook.* New York: Springer Publishing.

Villapando, O. (2003). Self-segregation or self-preservation? A critical race theory and Latina/o critical theory analysis of a study of Chicana/o college students. *International Journal of Qualitative Studies in Education, 16*(5), 619-646.

Villenas, S. (2001). Latina mothers and small-town racisms: Creating narratives of dignity and moral education in North Carolina. *Anthropology and Education Quarterly, 32*(1), 3-22.

Villenas, S., & Deyhle, D. (1999). Critical race theory and ethnographies challenging stereotypes: Latino families, schooling, resilience and resistance. *Curriculum Inquiry, 29*, 413-445.

Villenas, S. (1996). The Colonizer/Colonized Chicana ethnographer: Identity, marginalization, and co-optation in the field. *Harvard Educational Review, 66*(4), 711-731.

Wells, S. (2005, November 16, 2006). College dreams hang in the balance. Message posted to http://media.www.dailytarheel.com/media/storage/ paper885 /news /2006 /11/16/University/College.Dreams.Hang.In.Balance- 2463311 .shtml?sourcedo main=www.dailytarheel.com&MIIHost=media.collegepublisher.com

Willis, P. (1977). *Learning to labor : How working class kids get working class jobs.* New York: Columbia University Press.

Wolcott, H. (2001). *Writing up qualitative research.* Thousand Oaks, CA: Sage Publications.

Woodson, C. (1933).The *Mis-education of the negro.* New York: AMS Press.

Wortham, S., Murillo, E. G., Jr., & Hamann, E. T. (2002). *Education in the new Latino diaspora: Policy and the politics of identity.* Connecticut: Westport Publishing.

Yosso, T. (2006). *Critical race counterstories along the Chicana/Chicano educational pipeline.* Routledge: New York.

Younger, A. (2006), Living in the shadows. *Blue and White (November Issue 2006),* Retrieved on December 13, 2006 at http://www.unc.edu/bw/

Index